MORE PRAISE FOR

GOD IS MY BROKER

A *NEW YORK TIMES* BUSINESS BESTSELLER

"All that's missing here is the famous kitchen sink; what isn't missing, though, is enough humor for several volumes, and more than a few telling points."

—*San Francisco Examiner-Chronicle*

"Buckley and Tierney apply a wickedly deft touch in this laugh-out-loud funny 'self-help novel.'... The parodies and biblical puns slam into each other, piling up quickly in this satire-within-a-satire."

—*Boston Globe*

"A shrewd book.... Buckley and Tierney deserve credit for good timing as well as for their generally tart prose."

—*New York Times Book Review*

"Hilariously zany."

—*Publishers Weekly*

"*God Is My Broker* is great fun.... Scary, just like good satire ought to be."

—*Columbus Dispatch*

"*God Is My Broker* is a must-read for all the cynics who have come up with Brother Ty's Seventh Law of Spiritual and Financial Growth themselves while watching late-night, make-a-billion dollars, real estate commercials: 'The Only Way to Get Rich From a Get-Rich Book, Is to Write One.'"

—*Rocky Mountain News*

"Sending up self-help literature may be too easy, even redundant. But it sure is fun, and Buckley and Tierney have at least reached the ne plus ultra of logical absurdity in the genre: the intersection of self-help and moneymaking advice."
—*Worth*

"*God Is My Broker* does a terrific job of spoofing the self-help books that destroy so many trees."
—*Detroit News/Free Press*

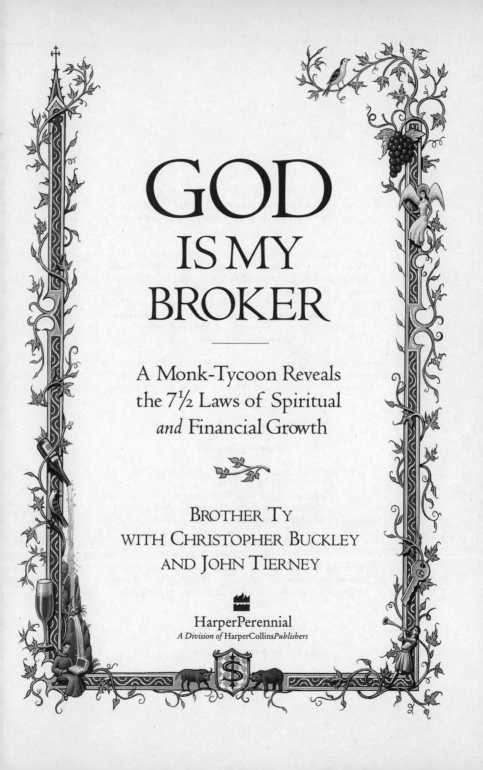

GOD
IS MY
BROKER

A Monk-Tycoon Reveals
the 7½ Laws of Spiritual
and Financial Growth

Brother Ty
with Christopher Buckley
and John Tierney

HarperPerennial
A Division of HarperCollins*Publishers*

First HarperPerennial edition published 1999.

Designed by Penny Blatt

Library of Congress Cataloging-in-Publication Data
Ty, Brother.
God is my broker : a monk-tycoon reveals
the 7½ laws of spiritual and financial growth /
Brother Ty with Christopher Buckley and John Tierney. — 1st ed.
p.   cm.
Originally published: New York : Random House, 1998.
ISBN 0-06-097761-2
1. Christian life—Humor.   2. Business—Religious aspects—
Christianity—Humor.   3. Monastic and religious life—Humor.
I. Buckley, Christopher, 1952–   .   II. Tierney, John Marion.
III. Title.
[BV4517.T9 1999]
813'.54—dc21   98-44946

99 00 01 02 03 ❖/RRD 10 9 8 7 6 5 4 3 2 1

Author's Note

At the end of each chapter of this book, you will find one of the Seven and a Half Laws of Spiritual and Financial Growth. Following each law is a Market Meditation designed to deepen your understanding of the Law. These "meditations" are principally the work of Christopher Buckley and John Tierney, whom the publisher brought in late in the process in an attempt, as they put it, to "punch up the material." It was not the easiest collaboration. While I have no doubt that Messrs. Buckley and Tierney are competent professionals, it takes delicacy to translate spiritual principles into universally understood lessons. We did not always agree on the wording of the "meditations," but the publisher explained more than once that these were "a necessity in today's personal growth book market." I took this to mean that the book would not otherwise be published. I acceded, but hope that the reader will understand that the techniques and examples—to say nothing of the sentiments—expressed in these "meditations" are not mine.

For reasons that will be clear, I have taken liberties with some facts in this narrative. Historians differ as to certain details of the life and writings of Saint Thaddeus of Thessaly. Rest assured, however, that every word quoted from the works of Deepak Chopra and other modern authors is strictly accurate, difficult as that may be to believe.

—*Brother Ty*
MONASTERY OF CANA

To the Abbot,

in the Knowledge
that God's Mercy and
Forgiveness Are Infinite

GOD
IS MY
BROKER

CHAPTER THE FIRST

Crisis in the Cloister…
The Abbot Gets a Guru…
A Heavenly Tip

 HE DAY BEGAN, AS ALL DAYS at the Monastery of Cana began, with the tolling of the bells and the shuffling of sandaled feet across a floor of cracked linoleum. In its day, it had been polished marble, but the marble had long since been sold to pay for necessities during our time of tribulation. By now we were well accustomed to poverty, but little did we know, on that cool September morning, just how dire our situation was.

It was the beginning of my second year, and I was excited at being allowed to speak again after the traditional year of silence.

All during that year I had wondered, silently, what my fellow brothers made of me. I had traded the life of a Wall Street broker for the contemplative life, my briefcase for a rosary, the roar of the trading floor for Gregorian chant. Once, as I was on my knees scrubbing the linoleum (taking care not to brush too hard lest I crack it further), I heard Brother Fabian tell Brother Bob: "I guess 'Brother Tycoon' bought high and sold low!" That one playful gibe caught on, and my nickname among the other monks became Brother Ty. My vow of silence never chafed so painfully, but then I reminded myself that this was why I had sought sanctuary from the grasping world. And, if truth be told, they were not far off the mark. As my managing director had said to me the day I was dismissed from the firm, "This has been one of the greatest bull markets in history. How did you manage to lose so much of our clients' money?" I had no answer. I walked out and headed up the Street to Slattery's Bar.

"Top of the morning," said Slattery. "The usual?"

My *usual*? How many mornings *had* I spent here, reading the *Journal* while knocking back Bloody Marys?

"Slattery," I replied, "let me ask you, as a friend: is it your opinion that I have a drinking problem?"

He looked at me thoughtfully. "Well, does it interfere with your job?"

"Not anymore," I said truthfully.

That was about as much as I recall of that day. I came to lying on my stomach in a storage room next to a case of bottles labeled "Cana 20-20." With some difficulty, and not a little pain, I ascended to my knees and inspected a bottle, which seemed to contain red wine with an orangish tinge. I unscrewed the cap and took a sip. Suddenly I became convinced, without ever having sampled a mixture of grape Kool-Aid and battery acid, that it would taste precisely like the fluid now in my mouth. I spat it on the floor and careened to the men's room to rinse out the gritty residue. I was staring into the mirror, picking what appeared to be particles of rust from my teeth, when Slattery found me. He was closing up for the night, but I begged for a cup of coffee to wash away the taste. He poured it at the bar.

"You know," he said as I scalded myself trying to drink the coffee, "maybe you aren't cut out for Wall Street. Watching you in here mornings, I got the feeling all you wanted was to get away from the Big Board. You don't need a bottle to do that."

His words burned into me even more than the coffee, although not quite as much as the wine. Perhaps after all I wasn't meant for the Street.

"Get away from here," he urged. "Get out into the country. Remember what grass looks like?" He pointed to a calendar showing what looked at this distance like a country field with cows. Or maybe sheep. I was in no position to distinguish between things bright and beautiful.

"Are those sheep or cows?" I mumbled.

"Those are monks, you blind drunk."

"Oh, right." It was a pastoral scene. Monks, doing something pastoral. Maybe with sheep. I was still in no position to judge.

"Why monks?" I asked.

He shrugged. "Those are the ones who make Cana 20-20."

I shuddered and washed some coffee down my throat. "I spilled some of that in the back room. Sorry. I'll clean it up."

"Awful stuff," said Slattery. "I couldn't serve it here. I give it to the winos. But it's a nice place and they're good souls and what the hell, it's a good cause, right?"

"What," I said, "are you talking about? The sheep or the monks?" By now the old windows of the soul were defogged to the point where I could make out the scene on the calendar. In the background, above the monks in the vineyard, was a brick building and a church on a green hill. "It does look like a nice spot."

"I visited it after my wife died," Slattery said. "They have rooms for guests—nothing fancy, just a bunk. Most peaceful vacation of my life. You might like it. Although I guess a winery isn't exactly the place for you these days."

"Slattery," I said, "they could serve that stuff at the Betty Ford Center and no one would drink it."

Slattery smiled as I washed down more coffee. "Well," he said, "maybe Cana *is* the place for you."

"How far is it from Wall Street?"

"Couple hundred miles," said Slattery. "If you hit Canada, you've gone too far."

I didn't hit Canada. And the week in the Monastery of Cana's guesthouse turned into two years. The vacation became a vocation.

IT WAS COMFORTING, that September morning as I chanted with the other monks, to feel so far from the material world, with all its getting and spending and so little getting of understanding.

I was, after the usual custom, about to go out and check the vines for overnight frost, when the Abbot made a special announcement.

"Before going to your duties," he intoned, "assemble in the calefactory.[1] I have something to say to you."

We gathered around the folding card tables pushed together to approximate the shape of the magnificent fifteenth-century Florentine table that we had sold in order to repair the roof.

Brother Bob, sitting next to me, said under his breath, "Another announcement. What is there left to sell? Us?"

The Abbot stood before us, a picture of exhaustion. A barrel-chested man in his mid-fifties, he had normally a booming baritone voice and a hearty manner that cheered us all through the long winters, doubtless the same quality that had made him a legendary captain of the Holy Cross football squad. But this morning, in the dim predawn light, the usually ruddy face looked drawn and fatigued. The strain of fending off bill collectors and watching the monastery literally fall apart had taken its toll. Of late he had been acting erratically; some of the older monks whispered that he had been muttering obscenities in Latin. Now there was something in his eyes I had never seen before: a look of desperation.

"Brothers," he addressed us, "I will begin with the good news. There can be little doubt that we have lived up to our vow of poverty." He held up a fistful of cash. "We have $304. Our bank account is empty. Our credit is exhausted. We

---

[1] Calefactory. From the Latin for "heated room," traditionally where the monks gather to talk by the fire.

have nothing of value left to sell." He sighed. "Unless the antiques dealers suddenly develop an interest in our vintage linoleum floor. We have one functioning vehicle left, with a quarter tank of gas. We have no hopes of attracting re-treatants to be our guests unless we do something about the plumbing and—through no fault of Brother Tom—our food." For the last four months we had been surviving on food stamps and cases of canned succotash and beets that, we had been told by their donor, had fallen off some semi-trucks on the Interstate.

"I have appealed once again to our superiors at the Vati-can." Our monastery was the last remnant of a once flour-ishing order, the Order of Saint Thaddeus. Our founder, a fervent twelfth-century penitent who was eventually mar-tyred by Sultan Omar the Magnanimous, had put the order under direct authority of the Pope. But our relations with the Holy See in Rome had been strained ever since an un-fortunate incident ten years before. As per tradition, the monastery had sent the first case of the new wine to the Pope. His Holiness took ill shortly after drinking a glass with his dinner. Although it was never conclusively proved that our wine had caused his distress, the chemical analysis turned up a number of "impurities."

"The Vatican was once again disinclined to offer financial assistance," the Abbot said. "My warning that we would have to shut down our winery was not greeted with alarm. And, frankly, who can blame them?"

The Abbot spoke as though struggling to maintain con-trol. "Our wine-making machinery is hopelessly antiquated. Due to our problems with quality control, the Cana label has been dropped by every wine distributor except the one owned by Brother Theodore's uncle. And now even his devotion and loyalty are wavering. Uncle Leo called me yesterday after sampling the Cana Nouveau. He is a kind man. I got the feeling that his charity is being sorely tested."

"What did he say?" asked Brother Theo.

"He described in some detail the difficulty he had swallowing it. Though he does not wish to abandon us, he said that he knew of no liquor store in America, even in the least fortunate neighborhoods, or for that matter, anywhere in the industrialized world, that would buy Cana from him, at any price. He asked me if we had ever considered marketing it as an industrial solvent. I assured him that he must have received a bad batch. At any rate, he is coming next week to taste the new vintage, and I do not think we can try his faith any further. The Lord does not expect us to produce wine from water, but we ought to be able to make it from grapes. If we can't do that, we'd better find some other business, because when the $304 is gone, so will Cana be gone."

There was a deep silence, deeper even than the normal monastic silence. Brother Algernon spoke: "You mean, close the monastery?"

"The rules of the Order of Saint Thaddeus require us to be self-sufficient. I doubt Saint Thad would rejoice if he knew that we have been living on food stamps. Winter is coming. I still haven't paid last year's fuel-oil bill. Unless you have a plan for alternative heat sources, we face a winter without heat, which is not an agreeable prospect in a climate where the temperature normally dips to ten below. None of us took a vow of lunacy. Or hypothermia."

I tried to dispel the gloom. "Perhaps we could use the wine to run the furnace."

My attempt at levity met with silence. Some of the brothers gave me disapproving looks.

"Would that work?" said Brother Jerome hopefully. Brother Jerome, who tended the pigs and hens, was known for his simplicity as well as his piety.

The Abbot sighed heavily, as he usually did when Brother Jerome offered one of his helpful suggestions. "We'll give that prayerful consideration. I think Brother Ty was making an attempt at humor. Perhaps his one year of silence was not sufficient." He glowered at me. "Brother, would you see me in my office. After you help Brother Jerome clean the sty."

He led us in a short prayer and bade us go about our duties. I went off to clean out the pigs' pen in penitential silence. That done, I went to see the Abbot.

He was deep in reading, sitting at his desk, an old door straddling two drab metal filing cabinets. "Oh, Brother Ty." He closed the book. He caught me reading the title.

CREATING AFFLUENCE
Wealth Consciousness
in the Field of All Possibilities
Deepak Chopra, M.D.

"Ever heard of this fellow?" He read aloud from the book jacket: " 'With clear and simple wisdom, Deepak Chopra explores the full meaning of wealth consciousness and presents a step-by-step plan for creating affluence and fulfillment on all levels of our lives.' His books have sold millions. They tell me he's on television all the time on the educational channel."

"You're not seriously—" I caught myself. It was clear from the poor man's face that he *was* serious. He was at the end of his tether. Best humor him, I decided. "Any lilies in this Field of All Possibilities?"

"I haven't gotten to the field part yet. He's got this system called 'The A-to-Z Steps to Creating Affluence.' It's either extremely profound, or—"

"Total rubbish?"

"To be honest, I had an easier time understanding Aquinas. I have no idea what the man is talking about. That's why I asked to see you. You worked with wealthy people on Wall Street. I understand Chopra has quite a following. What do *you* make of him?"

"Well," I said, trying to deflect the question, "I doubt he has much practical advice on wine-making."

"Let's look under W," he said, flipping. He read aloud:

> *"W stands for Wealth Consciousness without worries.*
> *Wealth consciousness implies absence of money worries.*
> *Truly wealthy people never worry about losing their*
> *money because they know that wherever money comes from*
> *there is an inexhaustible supply of it.*
>
> *"Once, when we were discussing a world peace project*
> *with my teacher, Maharishi Mahesh Yogi, somebody asked*
> *him, 'Where is all the money going to come from?' And*
> *he replied without hesitation, 'From wherever it is at the*
> *moment.'"*

The Abbot glanced at the price sticker on the back of the book with a look of despair. "I paid $14 for this. That money is on its way to Deepak Chopra. That is where *my* money is at the moment. The question is how to get it to come back."

I said, "Maybe you should have spent the $14 on a bottle of wine. For that, you could get something without rust particles in it."

"You're probably right. I should have gone to the liquor store instead. Certainly that is where the good wine is at the moment."

Suddenly his expression changed. He stared at the text with renewed intensity. " *'From wherever it is at the moment … From wherever it is at the moment.'* "

He stood. "Brother Ty, I have an errand for you."

I FOUND MYSELF puzzling over the Abbot's mutterings as I drove our '78 Ford pickup into town. He had handed me Cana's last $304 and instructed me to go to the liquor store and spend it on six cases of "decent Chilean table wine." I kept telling myself that he most likely wanted to analyze it in order to improve our own stuff. But as the chassis vibrated along the country road, the question nagged at me: why does he need so much wine to do that? *"Wherever it is at the moment."* It sounded like what Willie Sutton said to the judge when asked why he robbed banks. "That's where the money is."

Surely the Abbot had nothing improper in mind. The Abbot of the monastery named after Our Lord's first miracle wouldn't turn one wine into another. Surely we should be trying to improve our own wine, rather than putting someone else's wine in our bottles—just to fool Uncle Leo. Anyway, we could hardly afford to buy enough "decent Chilean table wine" to keep our customers deceived for long. The Abbot, I reassured myself, was a holy man, a pious man, a good man who had given up a promising career as a professional football player to lead the contemplative life. I calmed myself by meditating on my vow of obedience.

At the top of a hill, I heard a loud grinding sound in the vicinity of the transmission, followed by smoke. I pulled over. A passing motorist was kind enough to call a garage on his cellular phone. An hour later I found myself sitting disconsolately in Clark's Garage as Clark wiped the oil from his face and told me that a new transmission would cost $650. I showed him my $304, explaining that this represented the sum total of Cana's worth. He took pity on me and went to work. "I'll try," he said, "but I can't guarantee we'll be able to find parts for an antique like this."

I called the monastery and gave the Abbot the news. He did not take it well. He kept repeating, "What about the wine? What about the wine?" I was not getting through.

Suddenly he issued a torrent of language such as I had not heard since my days on the trading floor on Wall Street. My heart went out to the man. The stress was getting to him. I tried to calm him down as best I could, even making a little jest: "At least now we know where our money is at the moment." He did not laugh. There was a loud clatter that sounded like the phone dropping onto linoleum.

"Hello?" I said. Nothing. "Hello?"

A moment later, the voice of Brother Felix came on, full of concern. "What did you tell the Abbot?" I explained about the transmission and the $304.

"I wouldn't bother him any more today," Brother Felix whispered. "He has not taken your news well."

"What is he doing?"

"He has taken off his cincture[2] and is using it to flagellate a book."

"I think I know what book."

"I'd better attend to him," said Brother Felix, and hung up.

Clark called a parts distributor and, after being put on hold for five minutes, turned on the speakerphone and went back under the hood. The speaker blasted annoying music from the kind of radio station that calls itself progressive. These days it would not do to torture an American consumer on the phone with silence.

It was going on noon, time to take out my breviary, the prayer book that we always carry. Seven times a day, at regular hours, we recite our "Office," the daily cycle of prayers: Matins, Prime, Terce, Sext, None, Vespers, and Compline. I took out my breviary, looked up the noon reading for today and tried to recite it silently. I had to struggle through the din of the speakerphone.

I remember the moment vividly. I was trying to concentrate on the lines concerning Our Lord's driving the demons out of a possessed man—the poor Abbot came to mind— when a radio announcer's voice boomed out of the speakerphone. It was a voice from my past, the voice of Wall Street, full of urgency.

"There could be some swings this afternoon after the USDA report on farm output, with special volatility in pork bellies."

I tried to ignore the voice on the phone. *Get thee behind me, Satan,* I commanded it. I returned to my breviary and read

---

[2] Cincture: a length of heavy rope worn around the waist as a belt.

about the demons being driven out of the possessed man.
There on the page in front of me were the following words:

> *And the unclean spirits went out, and entered into the*
> *swine: and the herd ran violently down a steep place into*
> *the sea (they were about two thousand;) and were choked*
> *in the sea.*[3]

Now something possessed *me*. "Can I use this phone?" I
asked Clark.

My old friend Bill was surprised, to say the least, to get
my collect call.

"Jesus Christ," he practically shouted, "is that true about
you being in a monastery?"

I told him it was; he apologized for his language. I came
straight to the point: "Bill, I know you were always good
about giving. Well, here's your chance to help old Mother
Church." I explained about Cana's finances. Then: "I've got
a very hot tip that pork bellies are about to go off the cliff."

Bill's excitement was palpable. He yawned. "Is this as hot
as all your other tips?"

"Bill," I said, "I know my track record isn't the best. But
this source is different."

"Have you been drinking again?"

"Bill, I haven't had a drop in two years. You wouldn't want
to drink the stuff we make. That's the whole point."

"What do you mean?"

"Never mind. I swear to you two things. One, I'm sober.
Two, this is the monastery's only shot. I need to borrow two
grand for one afternoon."

---

[3] Mark 5:13.

"Two *grand*?"

"Bill, that's lunch money to you."

There was a long pause. Finally, he said, "I'll consider this an early Christmas donation. Okay now, you want to short pork bellies two thousand?"

"Yes." I tried to sound confident as we worked out the details of betting that the price of pork bellies on the commodities exchange would plummet.

"All right," he said. "Done. Where do I reach you?"

BY THE TIME Clark located the right parts it was late afternoon. The truck wouldn't be ready until the next day, so I hitchhiked back to Cana. I got a ride pretty quickly. Most people will brake for hitchhiking monks.

I went immediately to the Abbot's cell. A group of monks were standing outside it with looks of great concern. They told me that the Abbot's condition had worsened in the hours following my phone call. After flagellating the book, he had apparently hurled it into the fireplace, shouting, *"Ego te expello!"*[4] He had to be restrained from leaping into the fire after the book. It was then they decided to call Dr. Cooke, a sympathetic psychiatrist who worked at one of the nearby prisons. He was in with him now. Brother Felix said, "Dr. Cooke used the phrase 'reality disruption.' I think it's what we used to call a nervous breakdown."

I kept vigil with the brothers, offering up my poor prayers for the Abbot's recovery. I rebuked myself for not fully real-

---

[4] Latin for "I expel you!" Traditionally used in the Church while performing exorcisms or setting fire to heretics.

izing what a strain he had been under, and for not anticipating the result of my phone call.

At last, Dr. Cooke emerged from the cell. "I've given him an injection," he said. "He's a strong man, so you'd better watch him. He's calmed down now, but he keeps repeating something: 'That is where it is at the moment.' Is that from one of your prayers?"

The monks shook their heads. I decided it would be best not to illuminate the Abbot's meditation.

Just then Brother Algernon came to tell me there was an urgent phone call for me. It was Bill.

"Well, Brother, you got some good sources up there in that monastery. Bellies took a dive, just like you said."

"How much of a dive?"

"As of the bell, you're up $27,000. What name do you want on the account?" He paused. "Still planning to share it with the monastery?"

I hung up, stunned. This was the first decent stock tip I'd ever gotten, and it had come from—God. The Lord had heard our prayer, and provided. I have always been careful with the word "miracle," but how else to explain what happened this afternoon at Clark's garage?

I rushed to tell the Abbot the good news, hoping this would lift him from the depths of despair.

"Father Abbot?" I entered his cell. He was sitting up in bed with a strange glassy expression on his face. "How are you feeling?"

"Bene. Et tu?"[5]

---

[5] Latin: "Good. And you?"

I had never heard him speak conversational Latin before. I made a clumsy stab at a reply. *"Dominus vobiscum."*[6]

He spoke for some time, either about the weather or the transmission. My Latin being what it was, I could only nod sympathetically and interject an occasional *"Certe!"*[7] Finally I said to him, "Father, I have wonderful news."

"Quid?"[8]

"Could we speak English? Just for a moment?"

"Lingua Latina lingua Dei est."[9]

"I'm sure it is, but I don't know the word for pork bellies in Latin."

"Abdomina porcorum."

"Why don't I come right to the point," I said. "I know this might sound blasphemous, but I was reading my Office at the garage when I was inspired to take a gamble on the market. I called an old friend of mine and talked him into betting $2,000 that pork bellies were about to go sharply down in value. And guess what—it happened."

"Quid?"

"We made $27,000."

"QUID?"

"Here, let me write it out for you." I took the pad next to his bed and put down:

$MMMMMMMMMMMMMMMMMMMMMMMMMMMM

He began to mumble. I leaned closer. He was counting, in Latin. He looked up at me. "Twenty-seven thousand... *dollars?"*

---

[6] "The Lord be with you." Pretty basic Latin.
[7] "Certainly!"
[8] "What?"
[9] "Latin is the language of God."

I nodded. "It's in an account in our name at my friend's firm on Wall Street."

The Abbot's eyes widened. "So *that's* what he meant!"

"Who meant?"

"Deepak Chopra. *That* was where our money was at the moment! Wall Street!" He smiled. I shall never forget that smile.

"What are you talking about?" I said nervously. "God showed me the way, not Deepak Chopra, M.D. It was in the noon reading today. The story of the Gadarene swine. In our own breviary. Not in that silly book you threw in the fire."

"The fire!" the Abbot shrieked. He jumped out of bed and ran out of his cell before I could restrain him.

"The book!" he shouted. "The book!"

He ran into the calefactory, knocking over Brothers Felix and Bob, and began madly pawing through the ashes in the fireplace. "The book! Where is the book?"

Brother Felix asked, "Why do you want the book, Father Abbot?"

"That book saved our monastery!"

Brother Felix whispered to me, "We retrieved the book. We thought it might help the doctor with his diagnosis."

The Abbot was still shoveling ashes onto the linoleum. "Better let him have it," I said. The book was charred and burned away at the edges. The cover was slightly altered:

EATING AFFLUENCE

"Here, Father Abbot," said Brother Felix, holding it out to him.

The Abbot took it gently, as if it were a Dead Sea Scroll. He sat down and carefully turned to a page he seemed to recognize. He read aloud: " 'In order to acquire wealth you must intend it. The universe handles the details, organizes and orchestrates opportunities.' "

I held up my breviary. "But it was *this* book that gave me the inspiration."

"And who sent you on that mission?" replied the Abbot. "I intended you to make money. *And the universe handled the details.*"

I argued with him, to no avail. He took the book with him back to his cell. A great change had come over him—although at the time we had no idea just how great. But I already knew that our own lives would never be the same, for that day God had revealed Himself to be our broker. Next to the speakerphone in Clark's Garage I had learned the First Law of Spiritual and Financial Growth:

I.

IF GOD PHONES, TAKE THE CALL.

Market Meditation
the First

How many times have I put God "on hold"?
Has God ever put me "on hold"?
Is God ever out of cell phone range?
How can I screen out Satan's calls? Will Caller I.D. work?
Is a telephone the only way God has of calling me?
What if God calls collect?

You're asking very good questions. Now, as an exercise to help you master the Law, make a list of the times God has called you. (Hint: Did He use a phone?) For each call, fill out a pink WHILE YOU WERE OUT message slip describing the purpose of His call. Did you call back? Or did you decide it could wait until tomorrow? Calculate how much more money you would have if you'd called Him right back.

Now, ask yourself how much money you *lost* by taking Satan's calls. Think how much more you'd be worth now if you'd "screened out" his calls, or if you'd just told him, "I'll get back to you. We'll do lunch."

So, what have you found out from your calculations? You've lost a bundle, right? If time is money here on earth, imagine what it's worth in Heaven! Hint: you'll need one big calculator to figure *that* out!

Don't despair. After all, you bought this book, didn't you? Aren't you learning to return His calls right now?

Prayer of
the Prodigal Caller

*O Lord, Creator of the sky and the cables
that gird the earth, Router of all calls, grant that I
shall always be in to receive Thy calls,
and if I should not be in, grant me the wisdom
to get back to Thee immediately. Grant, too, that
I never play phone tag with Thee. Teach me to prioritize
all my communications, business and personal, so
that when day is done, there will be no urgent calls left
unmade. And may I always keep Thy
private number programmed on my speed dial.*

CHAPTER THE SECOND

First-Class All the Way…
An Unusual Rebuff…
A Second Call from
Our Broker

HE ABBOT REMAINED IN
seclusion for a week, studying
the collected works of Deepak
Chopra.

Despite this strange development, the mood in the rest of
the monastery had brightened.
For the first time in ages, Cana
had money in the bank. Between Gregorian chants, Brother
Bob whispered to me, "What will the Abbot do with all the
money?" I wondered myself. Twenty-seven thousand dollars was a lot of money to a group of monks on food stamps,
but to a winery that desperately needed to upgrade every
part of its operation, it was a pittance.

Finally the Abbot emerged. He looked rested, and seemed clearheaded, yet there was something different about him. He had a new air of confidence.

Where before he had been heartily stoic, taking problems as they came—until the problems overwhelmed him—now he seemed determined to meet troubles head-on. He also began hugging us, which unsettled Brother Bob somewhat.

At his first supper back with us, he ate quickly and moved to the lectern to read to us, as was the custom. I was eager to hear more from the book he had been reading us before his reality disruption, G. K. Chesterton's wonderful biography of Saint Thomas Aquinas, *The Dumb Ox*.

"Saint Thomas told us, 'Faith has to do with things that are not seen, and hope things that are not in hand.' " The Abbot stopped, deep in thought. " 'Hope for things that are not in hand.' How true, as we learned last week. We must have hope that things will come to us, from wherever they are."

The phrase stopped me in mid-swallow.

Smiling enigmatically, the Abbot reached into his cassock and took out a charred book. "Let us compare Saint Thomas's insights on hope with those of Dr. Chopra. Listen to what he has to say about things not yet *in* hand, but *at* hand."

Brother Bob shot me a look. He too had stopped chewing his stew. The Abbot read:

> "B stands for better and best. Evolution implies getting better and better in every way with time, ultimately getting for ourselves the best of everything. People with wealth consciousness settle only for the best. This is also called the

*principle of highest first. Go first-class all the way and
the universe will respond by giving you the best."* [10]

The Abbot looked up from his text at the monks, all of
whom had now stopped eating. "Let us keep these words in
mind as we go about our tasks."

On the way out, Brother Bob whispered to me, "Well,
there you have it, the evolution of moral philosophy, from
Thomas Aquinas to Deepak Chopra."

THE NEXT MORNING the Abbot summoned me. I was going
about my duties in the vat room, trying to scrape out the ac-
cumulated impurities in the vats.

The Abbot was at his desk, which was crowded with
items: bottles of Chilean cabernet sauvignon, copies of *Wine
Spectator* magazine, a jar of Newman's Own salad dressing,
more books by Deepak Chopra and other self-improvement
gurus.

"You wanted to see me, Father?"

"Ah, Brother Ty!" He came around the desk and hugged
me. "How *are* you?"

"We're working very hard to make this next batch at least
potable for Uncle Leo's tasting. But these rusty vats still
make it look a bit like Tang. Perhaps we could spend some of
the $27,000 on—"

"Never mind those vats," the Abbot said cheerfully.
"Making Cana drinkable would be beyond even our Lord's
abilities at this point. We've been going about this all wrong,

---

[10] *Creating Affluence* (1993), p. 28.

Brother. Why try to make rotten wine a little less rotten? True evolution means going for the best." He tapped Chopra. "First class! Highest first!"

"Well," I replied, "what sort of evolution do you have in mind? The Almighty created the heavens and earth in seven days, but"—I brushed some crud off my apron—"He didn't have to work with these vats."

The Abbot handed me a small glass of red wine. "Give me your prayerful opinion of this, Brother."

I sniffed. It smelled dismayingly good. "Delightful," I said. "I'd best not try it. I might like it too much. Obviously not from our own vineyard."

"Maipo Valley," said the Abbot. "Lovely part of Chile. Sunshine, good soil, *excellent* drainage. Far more suited to viticulture than upstate New York. *Fields* of possibilities, Brother."

"I'm not sure I understand. Are you proposing to relocate Cana to the Maipo Valley? On $27,000?"

"No," said the Abbot with a wily look. "We are going to move the Maipo Valley to Cana." He handed me a piece of paper.

At first glance I thought it was a copy of a page from an old illuminated manuscript. It was a fine piece of artistry—executed by our own Brother Algernon—in rich golds and burgundies, showing an ancient stone building looming over a vineyard where plump, cassocked figures were tending the vines. In the upper corner was a jolly, vaguely familiar face.

"Bacchus?" I asked.

"Read the label, Brother."

I made out the medieval calligraphy next to the face:

ABBOT'S OWN
Select Reserve Cabernet Sauvignon
From the Monastery of Cana

"Ah," I said. "It's you, Father Abbot. Quite a good like-ness." I stared at all the crenellated stone masonry on the label. "But I don't recognize the monastery. To my knowl-edge, Cana was not built in the fourteenth century. Nor have I noticed a moat in all my time here."

"Details," he said dismissively.

"God is in the details, according to Mies van der Rohe," I offered.

"The *universe* will handle the details, according to Deepak Chopra. I've been studying his work carefully over the past week, and now I see the big picture. How foolish of me to send you into town to pick up a couple of cases of Chilean wine. What a waste of your Wall Street skills. What we need here is—*volume.*"

He handed me an airline ticket. "This time, you're going where the wine really is."

THE WOMAN BEHIND the Lan-Chile counter looked up at me with surprise, and perhaps something else—a hint of contempt? It wasn't until she handed me back my boarding pass that I realized the Abbot had booked me first-class to Santiago.

"There must be some mistake," I said. "The order would never have bought a first-class ticket."

"No," she said clicking away at her computer screen, "they paid full fare for that—$5,580."

"But surely—" I stammered, aghast. Then it dawned on me—that line from Deepak Chopra: *Go first-class all the way and the universe will respond by giving you the best.*

Wonderful, I thought. Now I will spend the next eight hours sitting in first class, explaining to one and all that my vow of obedience takes precedence over my vow of poverty. *The Abbot made me do it.*

I slunk off to the first-class lounge. Oddly, I was the only monk there. I retreated into my breviary to read my Office. The text was taken from the Song of Solomon, chapter two: "As the apple tree among the trees of the woods, so is my beloved among the sons. I sat down under his shadow with great delight, and his fruit was sweet to my taste. He brought me to the banqueting house, and his banner over me was love. Stay me with flagons, comfort me with apples."

Just as I was reading those words I overheard a business-man behind me telling his companion, "I dumped all my Apple today."

"I thought computer stocks were doing okay," said the other.

"Not Apple's. Their quarterly report is coming out to-morrow. Word on the street is it's going to be Hiroshima City. They're getting hammered on market share."

I reread the text: *Comfort me with apples.* It sounded like a "buy" recommendation to me. The Lord seemed to have more faith in Apple Computer's quarterly report than this fellow.

I ran off to the nearest phone and telephoned Cana. I told the Abbot that I thought Our Broker was bullish on Apple. "Maybe He wants us to leverage our $27,000 with options on Apple."

"Take out the book," said the Abbot serenely, "and turn to page thirty-seven."

Obediently, I opened my breviary. Page 37 was entirely devoted to Saint Thad's detailed instructions for the proper mortification of the flesh.

"Okay, I'm on page thirty-seven. Saint Thad on cold baths? Going barefoot on hot coals?"

"Not that book. The book I gave you with your ticket."

Obediently I took out *Creating Affluence* and turned to page 37. I whispered into the receiver so that no one would hear me: " 'I' stands for the power of unbending intent or intention. It is to make an unchangeable decision from which it is impossible to go back."

"Get on that plane," the Abbot said. "And get your mind off apples. Apples are nothing but trouble. 'Ye shall not eat of it, neither shall ye touch it.' Genesis 3:3. Good-bye, Brother Ty."

I went back to my seat. A few minutes later there was an announcement. "We regret to inform our first-class passengers aboard Flight 40 that our four-thirty departure has been delayed due to an equipment problem. At this time, our new estimated departure time is . . . twelve o'clock."

The businessman behind me who had dumped his Apples jumped up and disappeared. A moment later he could be heard lecturing the first-class lounge attendants on the deficiencies of Chilean technology and character.

"If I'm not at the Santiago Hilton by ten A.M. *mañana,* I am going to lose more money than you will ever make in your life, and I will sue Lan-Chile, and you personally. *COMPRENDE, SEÑORITA?*" He came back and kicked over a coffee table.

Trying to soothe him, I said, "Perhaps this is God's way of telling you that the meeting at the Hilton isn't really that important. Maybe He has something even bigger in store for you."

The man looked at me in disbelief. He took in my monk's habit.

"Fuck *off,* Father," he said.

As the unusual phrase "Fuck off, Father" resonated in my ears, I decided that this lounge was not the most congenial place in which to spend the next eight hours, so I took a taxi into the city, thinking to visit awhile with Slattery.

Pulling up in front of my old haunt, I remembered all those early mornings walking in with trembling hands to have the first snort of the day.

Slattery was there. So was Bill. Heads turned as I walked in. Slattery said, "If it isn't the Second Coming."

I sat down, ordered a seltzer water, and asked Bill what was new.

"Everyone's dumping Apple," he said.

"So I hear," I said. We made idle chat for a few minutes, I ordered a sandwich, and then asked Slattery if I could stash my bag in the back. I had a sense of déjà vu as I walked into the room where my new journey had begun two years ago. There were still a few cases of Cana 20-20 stacked up.

Then it hit me: wine...flagons. Slattery's...banqueting house.... I took out my breviary and reread: *He brought me to the banqueting house...stay me with flagons, comfort me with apples.*

I rushed back in and sat down next to Bill. I pulled out the $20,000 cashier's check intended for the purchase of Chilean wine, and my $5,580 round-trip first-class ticket.

"Bill," I said, "I want $25,000 worth of Apple calls."[11]

Bill looked at me incredulously. Why would I be betting that Apple stock was going to rise, when everyone on the Street thought it would plunge.

"No, you don't," he said.

"Yes, I do."

"Look, we hear that their quarterly tomorrow is going to be gruesome. The *last* thing you want is Apple calls."

Comfort me with apples.

I knew the Lord was telling me to buy Apple, but it definitely wasn't going to be comfortable.

I looked Bill in the eye and said, "Do it. This comes from the same source as the bellies tip."

Bill looked dubious. "This guy knows pork bellies *and* tech stocks?"

"This Guy knows everything."

Bill leaned in and whispered, "How did you find this guy? He live upstate?"

"He has a home there," I said.

Bill shook his head. "I guess he's got a lot of homes. Nothing personal, but why is he giving you all this? He a big Catholic or something?"

"Very big. Let's just say He looks after the monastery."

I handed him the $20,000 check.

"You want the whole twenty thousand in Apple calls?"

"Plus this," I said, handing over the Lan-Chile ticket.

Bill stared at it. "You were going to Chile? First-class?" He looked puzzled. "What, does he have another home there?"

---

[11] If you buy a "call" option, you are betting that the price of the stock will go up.

✠

I SPENT THE night in my old room at Slattery's among the cases of Cana—*Stay me with flagons!*—and the next day in church. I read my Office prayerfully, looking anxiously for any troubling references to rotten fruit. At noon I was sorely tempted to leave and call Bill to find out about Apple's report, but resolved to put myself in the Lord's hands, and trust in His market sense. Still, I was tormented: had I read His report correctly?

At four o'clock I raised myself from my knees and, somewhat stiffly, walked outside. What a contrast the Street was to the quietude of the church. I went to the nearest phone and dialed Bill. His secretary told me he was in a meeting, but when I told her my name, she said, "Oh, Brother Ty, please hold, I'll get him right away."

My stomach was churning. After an eternity, Bill came on.

"Jesus Christ," he said, "who *is* this guy? The quarterly caught everyone by surprise. They cut their losses, earnings are stable. The stock shot up six points. Your options are currently worth..." I heard him tapping his computer "...$462,000."

I called the Abbot.

"You're still in New York?" he said.

"Yes," I said, "but I think you'll forgive me. We have a little more in our account—462 Roman numeral M's, to be precise."

He shouted with joy: "We bought a first-class ticket and the universe has given us the best!"

I would tell him later about the true source of the stock tip. There was no point arguing with him now. He was too excited, and besides, even I had to admit that God seemed to want me in the first-class lounge. I had learned the Second Law of Spiritual and Financial Growth:

II.

GOD LOVES THE POOR, BUT THAT DOESN'T MEAN HE WANTS YOU TO FLY COACH.

Market Meditation
the Second

Could I use a little more "leg room" in my life?
Have I tried asking God for an upgrade to first class?
No room in first? How about business class?
No room in business, either?
Does God really want me on this flight?
Can you spell "destiny" without the d-e-s-t-i-n in "destination"?
Am I having an "equipment problem"?
Do I have God on my "maintenance team"?
Okay, there's no room in first, business, or coach,
and there's an equipment problem. Hello!
Is God trying to tell me something?
(Hint: remember the First Law about picking up the phone?)

Excellent—you're asking really good questions. As a wise man once put it, "A flight delayed does not necessarily mean a passenger dismayed." How about that jerk in the first-class lounge, dumping all his Apple stock and getting bent out of shape because he's not going to make it to the Santiago Hilton by 10:00 A.M. B-I-G D-E-A-L! He got hot, Ty stayed cool—and made a cool half mil. When the road of life gets rocky, maybe God is telling you to "chill out." Take out a pen and piece of paper. Write down this Essential Corollary™ to the Second Law™ and put it in your wallet:

IF YOU'RE GOING THE WRONG WAY—TURN AROUND!

Prayer of
the Inconvenienced Traveler

*O Lord, Supreme Travel Agent, who rerouted
Moses through the Red Sea, and found Mary and Joseph
accommodations on Christmas Eve, when they
had no reservation, grant that I should be
upgraded into the celestial kingdom of ample legroom,
where the beverages are complimentary and
the flight attendants answer the call button.*

CHAPTER THE THIRD

Philomena Arrives…
The Abbot Redecorates…
The Monks Film a
Commercial

E HAVE EATEN OF THE Apple," said Brother Bob, "and now Eve has arrived."

A month had passed. The Abbot had delved deeper into Deepak and assigned monks to study the other self-help gurus. He had postponed sending me to Chile to buy wine, and was instead concentrating on what he was calling the "repositioning" of Cana. There would be no more "thinking small," he announced, heading off to attend a seminar at a California resort with Deepak Chopra himself. I was stunned by the cost of this "retreat," as the Abbot called it. The official title in Chopra's brochure was "Journey to the Boundless," which I did not understand until I contemplated the bill: first-class (naturally) airfare, fees for the seminar and "educational materials," four days at the L'Extravaganza Spa and Resort—a total of $8,324.19. This was roughly what we had spent on food the previous year. I was even more stunned when the Abbot returned in a stretch limousine in the company of a most attractive female.

Her name was Philomena. She was in her early thirties. She had large, beautiful hazel eyes, short gamine hair, and a figure that those of my calling would best ignore. She was from Richmond, Virginia, originally, so she had the charm and the accent of a Southern woman; though also, it quickly became apparent, something of the steel of the Confederacy.

The Abbot had met her at the Chopra seminar. She was a management consultant with Beals-Bubb, the international firm based in New York City. She had been intrigued to find an abbot at a Chopra seminar, and he had been intrigued to find a follower of Chopra well schooled in marketing. He had hired her on the spot—for a fee that I blush to reveal, even now—to "maximize brand-name recognition of the Cana and Abbot's Own labels, with emphasis on identifying growth potential." There was nothing in the contract, I noticed, about actually improving our wine.

The Abbot formally introduced her to the monastic community at the noonday meal. There was some grumbling among the older monks about the presence of a woman. She gave a brief and, I must say, engaging account of her experience. She had been on the account team that had tripled Chrysler car sales in Japan.

"Japanese Chrysler dealers were reluctant to accept a woman on the team," she noted. "But they got used to it, especially after they saw what our marketing plan did for their sales." I admired her deftness. It was a delicate way of saying, *I know you're not used to skirts in the monastery, but give me a chance.* As she spoke, the Abbot nodded approvingly.

"If she can persuade the Japanese to drive American cars," he said, "she can surely convince Americans that Cana is drinkable."

Brother Bob raised his hand. "Is the plan to make the wine drinkable?"

"We're certainly looking at that," she said.

"Right," said the Abbot, "let's not get bogged down in the details. Now, Philomena, it's customary to have someone read to us during our meals. Would you care to do the honors? Perhaps one of the texts we studied at the seminar? *The Seven Spiritual Laws of Success?*"

"If it would be appropriate," she said demurely, "I'd like to read from something else, a book that has meant a lot to me." She reached into her briefcase and produced a dog-eared paperback. "Here it is. *The Thorn Birds.*"

The Abbot looked startled. "Ah. Fine. You're fond of the book?"

"I've read it eight times."

"Ah."

The monks exchanged glances.

Philomena chose a section dealing with a financial dilemma of the novel's handsome priest: whether to accept an extraordinarily large sum of money bequeathed to him and the Church by an elderly woman, or whether to allow the money to go instead to the woman's hardworking relatives. Philomena read to us of the priest's tormented decision to accept the money. The Abbot was so enthralled with this moral lesson that he asked her to continue with the next scene. Philomena demurred, but the Abbot insisted, so we heard about the tormented priest's horseback ride with one of the disfranchised relatives, a beautiful teenaged niece named Meggie.

It became uncomfortably clear to all of us that the priest's vow of chastity was being tested by the teenager. Philomena's mellifluous voice became hushed as she read the priest's admonition to the girl: "What you mustn't do is get into the habit of dreaming about me in any sort of romantic fashion. I can never regard you the way a husband will. I don't think of you in that light at all, Meggie, do you understand me? When I say I love you, I don't mean I love you as a man. I am a priest, not a man."

Philomena continued reading about the priest's attempt to console the girl by putting his arm around her:

> "Though he held her, he did not have any intention of kissing her. The face raised to his was nearly invisible, for the moon had set and it was very dark. He could feel her small, pointed breasts low down on his chest; a curious sensation, disturbing. Even more so was the fact that as naturally as if she came into a man's arms every day of her life, her arms had gone up around his neck, and linked tightly."

The Abbot coughed gently and rose to his feet. "Very nice. Thank you, Philomena. And now we all have work to do."

PHILOMENA TOOK UP residence at a nearby motel, meeting with us daily to go over her marketing plan. Our sessions took place in the Abbot's cramped, decrepit office, which Philomena one day jokingly called "the executive suite." To me it seemed a casual remark made in good fun, but it planted a notion in the Abbot's head.

"You know," he remarked to me later, "Philomena is right."

"About what?"

"We should have an 'executive suite.' Look at this," he said, indicating the rotting door that served as his desk, the dilapidated file cabinets, the manual typewriter, the crumbling plaster walls. "This is not first-class, Brother Ty."

"It seems fine to me," I replied. "I don't think she meant anything by it."

"I think Philomena would like a more dignified place to work."

"I'm not sure I understand," I said warily. "Is it that Philomena wants a bigger office, or you want a bigger office. Or do you want a bigger office for Philomena?"

"You're getting bogged down in details." He wagged a finger at me. "How do you expect us to fit the Field of All Possibilities in this . . . closet?"

I feared that the Abbot was contemplating going to somewhat elaborate lengths to impress Philomena, an increasingly popular pastime at Cana these days. The monks were paying more attention to their appearance of late: pressing their cassocks, knotting their cinctures smartly. Even

Brother Jerome's socks matched. One day, as we were in chapel chanting Saint Thad's paean to pain, *De Doloribus Extremis*,[12] Brother Bob nudged me and pointed at the row of monks in front of us. "Notice anything different?"

As I sang Saint Thad's verse about rolling around in bramble bushes, I looked. Something did seem out of place—but what? Then it dawned on me: the distinctive bald spots on the backs of the monks' heads—called tonsures—had all but disappeared.

"Behold, the Cana Comb-over," whispered Brother Bob.

Philomena seemed bemused when the Abbot told her that he wanted to expand his office and asked for her advice on how to go about it.

She demurred. "Interior design isn't really my area. If you saw my apartment"—she laughed—"you wouldn't ask my advice on decor."

The Abbot touched her arm tenderly, "I would value *any* advice from you," he said. "Because of your efforts, Cana will be expanding. We're going to be spending a lot of time working here. And I want you to be happy."

Philomena blushed. I broke the silence by humming from *De Doloribus*. It occurred to me that perhaps the Abbot needed a good roll in the bramble bushes.

"I'll see if I can get you the name of someone," she said. And so it came to pass, one week later, that Elliott entered our lives.

Elliott arrived in a black sedan, dressed head to toe in black, including heavy black-frame glasses that, I noticed,

[12] Latin: "On Extreme Pains."

had no lenses. "When you have a face like mine," he explained, "you've got to accessorize." It seemed a perfectly normal face to me, but perhaps my aesthetic standards were not as finely tuned as his. He had recently relocated his interior-design business from Soho, the downtown part of New York full of art galleries and lofts. Apparently it was no longer sufficiently hip for Elliott. "Soho," he explained, "is NoMo." His new offices were in a former slaughterhouse in the meat district. "I love unusual spaces," he said. "When Philomena said it was a monastery, I said, 'I'm there.'"

He seemed somewhat less thrilled now that he was "there." He toured Cana in silence. We sat down afterward in the Abbot's office, over tea.

"Well," Elliott said, taking a deep breath, "there are some interesting elements."

"Obviously," the Abbot said, "we haven't been concentrating on maintenance."

"You've been doing other things," said Elliott. He studied the cracked linoleum floor.

"That used to be marble," the Abbott said.

"I love old linoleum," said Elliott. "But I don't work with it."

The remark hung there for a moment. The Abbot said, "I see."

"Okay," said Elliott, resting his teacup on the cardboard box that served as a coffee table. "Let's begin with the good news." He looked out the window. "There's plenty of room to expand. I have clients who would kill for space like this. We can knock out the walls—with a hammer, probably. Plenty of room for—what are we talking about? Start with the basics—outer office, inner office. Conference area. Screening area—for the conferences. Atrium? We could do an atrium. With this light, you can't *not* do an atrium. There's nothing more soothing than a fountain. Would a prayer area be appropriate, or does that happen somewhere else? Actually," he said without waiting for an answer, "a prayer area could be quite interesting."

"I think the Abbot had something less extensive in mind," I ventured.

"Wait a minute," said Elliott. "I think we're forgetting something."

"Yes," I said, "the cost."

"The wine cellar! You make wine, right? That's what this place is all about—I mean, it's not *all* about wine, obviously. But it's your ... it's *what you do*. What was I thinking? Here I am—what's that line in the Bible?—hiding your lamp under a bush."

"Bushel," I said. "Hiding your light under a bushel."

"Brother, please," said the Abbot. He turned to Elliott. "What sort of overall ... feel did you have in mind?"

"Comfortable austerity," said Elliott. "We want it to say 'Poverty,' but we don't want it to say 'Cheap.' "

"CHEAP" IT CERTAINLY wasn't. The estimate for the Abbot's executive suite, now more of an executive complex, came in at $1.3 million. I pointed out that we did not have $1.3 million. I was castigated for small thinking, and told to find it, wherever it was.

The Abbot showed me a Deepak Chopra book called *The Seven Spiritual Laws of Success,* pointing out number four, the

Law of Least Effort: "Ultimately you come to the state where you do nothing and accomplish everything."

When I was unmoved by this earthshaking revelation, the Abbot brought out more books—Stephen Covey's *The Seven Habits of Highly Effective People* and Anthony Robbins's *Awaken the Giant Within.* "It may interest you to know, Brother, that the president of the United States had both these gentlemen to Camp David recently[13] to speak to the White House senior staff about how to run the government," the Abbot said.

When I still demurred, he handed me Norman Vincent Peale's *The Power of Positive Thinking.* "Perhaps you won't be so snooty about this one," he said. "It's one of the classic texts. It's sold over five million copies."

I took it back to my cell and tried reading it. There was an inspiring story about a door-to-door saleswoman who told herself, "If God be for me, then I know that with God's help, I can sell vacuum cleaners.' I stopped reading there, deciding to stick with our breviary.

With some more timely tips from Our Broker, I was gradually able to enlarge our portfolio. I spent many hours on the phone with Bill on Wall Street. He took to calling our account the Cana Hedge Fund.

Philomena completed her ambitious marketing plan. It was built around creating "name recognition" of the Cana label. Her idea was to create a television commercial using the monks themselves.

---

[13] December 30, 1994.

"Viewers respond to authenticity," she explained over the roar of the bulldozers excavating the foundation for the Abbot's wine cellar. "They love 'real,' and what could be more real than monks?"

She hired a director named Brent. Brent wore a jacket with lots of zippered pockets, and had a young female assistant.

"I'm not exactly religious myself," he said, by way of introducing himself, "but I respect what you're doing out here." To set us further at ease he said that he loved *The Name of the Rose.*

Brent had earned a Clio—the Oscar award of the TV commercial industry—for a successful lawn-care commercial featuring a rhinoceros. At first he was somewhat put out that we were not familiar with it, until Philomena pointed out that there was no television at Cana.

"No *TV?*" he said. "That's harsh."

A crew arrived from New York. Philomena and Brent set to work screen-testing the monks. Some of them were not sure they wanted starring roles in what they were calling around the calefactory *The Name of the Rosé.* The questions Brent put to them as they sat before him, sweltering and blinking under the hot lights, hardly helped: "Tell us a little about yourself. So why did you become a monk? Some adolescent trauma thing?" Nor did it help when, a few days into this grueling process, the young attractive assistant returned from New York with monastic robes identical with the ones worn in *The Name of the Rose.*

"Exactly what," I said to Brent sharply, "is wrong with our robes?"

"They're not doing it for me," he said.

"I'm sorry they don't meet with your approval," I said, "but these robes have been 'doing it' for our order since the year 1193."

"O-kay," said Brent to his crew in the weary tone of a patient director confronted with a prima donna. "Let's take a fifteen-minute break." He stomped off on loafered feet to smoke with his assistant.

Philomena held up one of the robes against me, like a clerk in a dress store. "It's you."

"I thought you said that viewers responded to authenticity. What's 'authentic' about these Hollywood costumes?"

"The viewers will just be responding to a different reality. The reality of the movie."

"Please."

"Think about it. How many people in America have ever seen a monk? It's not like you're constantly bumping into them at the mall." She put her hand on my shoulder. "Would it help to remind yourself that Brent is considered the Sydney Pollack[14] of the thirty-second spot?"

I confess that I was not thinking of Brent. It had been years since any woman had touched me. She was looking at me in a coquettish sort of way. I don't mean indecently— Philomena was not that sort of woman. She was simply humoring me and trying to get the job done, and yet I thought I detected something else in the look she gave me. This *was* a woman who had read *The Thorn Birds* eight times.

"Very well," I mumbled. I left her and Brent to the screen-testing, and went off to read Saint Thad's meditation

---

[14] Director of *Out of Africa* and *Tootsie,* among others.

on cleansing the soul through immersion in the gelid rivers of Cappadocia.

A FEW DAYS later she and Brent began filming their commercial. I was not surprised that the Abbot had managed to land himself the leading role. Brent declared that he "oozed authority" while "still being accessible" (whatever that meant). The role of sidekick had gone to our pig keeper, Brother Jerome, who had a quality Brent described as "uncomplicated."

"Action!" said Brent. Brother Jerome was up to his knees in a large vat, trampling grapes, as the Abbot stood nearby, writing in a book with a quill pen. A boom box next to the vat was playing Gregorian chant.

The Abbot walked out of the room. Brother Jerome pressed a button on the boom box, which began blasting "Staying Alive" by the Bee Gees. The idea was for Brother Jerome to start discoing in the vat, arm raised à la John Travolta. Just before the Abbot returned with a fresh quill, he would press the button. "Salve Regina" would play, and he would resume solemnly trampling the grapes.

The announcer's voice would say, "Cana, the Cabernet for all tastes."

The Abbot would then say, "We will serve no wine before it's divine."

In my opinion—which no one sought—the commercial could have used a rhinoceros.

Filming did not proceed well. Brother Jerome kept discoing to Gregorian chant, and solemnly trampling to disco. Then he took it upon himself—despite Brent's demands that he desist—to sing along with the Bee Gees. His Bee Gees falsetto was bad enough on "Staying Alive," but became unbearable chanting along to the thirteenth-century "Salve Regina."

"Cut!" said Brent. It was a word we heard often during four days of shooting. One day there were 126 "takes."

The Abbot became so flustered that he began flubbing his lines.

"We will wine no time—"

"Cut."

"We will serve no swine before their—"

"Cut."

Brent would huddle over his video monitor with Philomena and the assistants, and frown—expensively, as I knew in my capacity as monastery bursar.

Tempers grew short. The Abbot began hurling quill pens at the floor in disgust; Philomena and Brent argued loudly. Only Brother Jerome, up to his knees in grape mush for twelve hours a day, remained serene.

My own reserves were wearing thin. I had come to Cana to get away from the world, but now the world had come to Cana and was screaming "Goddammit, people!" Brent cursed one time too many and I went over the top.

"Cut!" I shouted.

All heads turned. Brent looked appalled at my appropriating his line. I strode onto the middle of the set. "Look here," I said sternly to the startled crew and Philomena. "This language is inappropriate. This is not Hollywood. This is a monastery consecrated to Our Lord's first miracle on earth."

"Well, excuse me," said Brent. "I had no idea. Was that the one where he walked on water? Why don't you demonstrate it for us. You've got a lake here. Why don't you go take a walk on it."

"You know as much about the Bible as a rhinoceros," I replied. "For your information, the miracle of Cana had nothing to do with walking on water. Allow me to enlighten you."

I opened my breviary and read:

> *And the third day there was a marriage in Cana of Galilee; and the mother of Jesus was there with Jesus and His disciples.*
>
> *And when they had drunk all the wine, Mary the mother of Jesus said unto Him, "They have no wine."*
>
> *And there were set there six water-pots, containing two or three firkins apiece.*
>
> *And Jesus said unto the servants, "Fill the pots with water." And they did.*
>
> *Jesus said, "Now take some and give it to the chief steward." The steward tasted it, but he knew not whence it came.*
>
> *The steward called over the host, and said unto him, "Every man sets out at the beginning of a feast his good wine, and then, when everyone has well drunk, that which is worse. But thou hast saved the good wine until now."[15]*

I looked up to see a half-dozen blank faces staring back at me.

[15] John 2:1–10

Philomena said, "So our slogan should be: 'Cana—the wine to serve when your guests are too drunk to know the difference'?"

"I could have used him at my daughter's wedding," Brent said, "but I don't see what the point is, frankly. We've got a commercial to make here."

"Wait a minute," Philomena said. "The miracle of Cana..."

TWO MONTHS LATER we assembled in the calefactory to watch the finished commercial. The Abbot proudly switched on the monastery's first videocassette recorder, which was hooked up to a new 128-inch television set. CANA MIR. I—30 SECONDS came on the screen, followed by the countdown to the commercial.

The screen filled with the scene of a modern wedding reception. A crowd of strikingly attractive, well-dressed people—Brent had cast this commercial outside the monastery—was laughing and dancing in a mansion's ballroom.

A grim-faced caterer approached the host, who was chatting with his daughter, the bride. The caterer whispered, "There's no wine left in your cellar."

The bride looked alarmed. The host reached into his pocket and pulled out a cell phone. He punched the buttons.

The scene shifted to the exterior of an old fortresslike monastery perched on a rocky crag, its turrets outlined against a range of snowcapped peaks. From inside came the sound of monks chanting, interrupted by the ringing of a phone. "Cana Monastery," a familiar voice answered.

Philomena, sitting in the audience next to the Abbot, nudged him.

Suddenly the oak doors of the monastery burst open, and a truck carrying a huge wooden wine cask labeled "Cana" rumbled across the drawbridge, with monks hanging on to the side, like firemen. It sped down the winding mountain road.

The truck screeched to a halt outside the mansion, where worried servants were waiting. A half-dozen monks hefted the cask off the truck and rushed inside.

The Abbot tapped the cask with a mallet, and wine poured forth. Waiters emerged bearing trays with full wineglasses.

The caterer held up a glass with delight. He slapped the host on the back. "You sly devil! You saved the best for *last!*"

The host beamed, looked off to the side, and winked.

The Abbot, standing by the cask, winked back, and turned to face the camera. Raising the glass to the viewer, he said merrily, "No, we saved the best for—thee!"

As the camera closed in tightly on the glass, the screen displayed 1-800-TRY-CANA. The Abbot's voice intoned, "The *new* miracle of Cana!"

We sat in silence for several seconds after the screen went dark. Then the Abbott rose to his feet and began applauding. About half the monks joined in. Several of the older monks bowed their heads and made the sign of the cross. I heard one behind me mutter, "Father, forgive them, for they know not what they do."

I couldn't help joining in the applause. I knew enough about Madison Avenue to appreciate a job well done. As much as Philomena's tactics offended me, I had to admire her talents—her smooth intelligence, her quick wit. She looked especially graceful as she took a bow at the Abbot's insistence. When he began praising her as a "first-class harvester in the Field of All Possibilities," she delicately interrupted him.

"I don't deserve all this credit. The idea came from Brother Ty."

The Abbot did not look pleased. I couldn't imagine why—surely he wasn't jealous of me? Philomena took note of his irritation.

"But mainly," she said, "the idea came from *you,* Father Abbot." The Abbot's face brightened.

To my surprise, I now found myself irritated. I knew it was vain to want credit for the idea, and I knew it was silly for me to begrudge Philomena's praise for the Abbot, yet it galled me to watch her cooing over him. What was going on between them?

After the screening, as the monks struggled to master the television's remote control, Brent came up and surprised me with a hug.

"You and that little book of yours really saved our bacon. You brought us up to a whole new level, man—Brother."

"Thank you, Brent," I said. He meant well. I tried to think of a return compliment. "Those robes of yours—they looked good. They did it for me."

Brent went off to hug someone else. I caught sight of Philomena and the Abbot having a spirited chat in the corner. He was leaning in closely, as if confiding a secret. It crossed my mind that there was precious little in the Chopran canon about chastity. I could hardly abandon the

Abbot to this occasion of potential sin. I walked over and joined them.

"Congratulations to you both on the commercial," I said heartily.

Philomena smiled; the Abbot did not seem overjoyed to be rescued. I pressed on, as tactfully as I could. "It's a brilliant piece of work. The turrets and the mountains looked great."

"Brent did a good job with the special effects and computer graphics," Philomena said.

"People are going to assume that's Cana," I said. "Do you think they'll be disappointed when they find out our monastery is not located—technically speaking—in the Alps?"

"Well…"

"But that's really secondary. The more interesting question is, how will they react when they find out that—technically speaking—we do not *have* any wine. Drinkable wine, that is. You know, the kind you would serve at a wedding reception."

The Abbot sighed. "Wherever small minds assemble, you will always have a place, Brother Ty."

He turned to Philomena. "I'm going back to my office to review the media buy. Could you join me there in a few minutes?"

After he left, I asked Philomena how long the Abbot had been using the phrase "media buy."

"Oh, he loves all this stuff," she said. "Actually, this is a fairly small buy—we only have two hundred grand left to spend. It's going to be tough to make an impact. Our best bet is probably to buy cheap time on the religious cable shows."

"You mean you're not going to advertise during *The Sound of Music*?" I said, trying to be sardonic.

"Why didn't I think of that! That's the *perfect* time slot." she said. She grabbed my hands and squeezed them.

"Philomena"—I tried again. "How can we market something we don't have? We're spending all our money on commercials. What about the wine? Where is the wine going to come from?"

"Ty," she said, "relax. We'll *get* the wine. Wine is not a problem. The world is drowning in wine. Have a little faith. You were the one who read us the Cana story. Remember the host? Did the host call off the party just because he didn't have any wine? Did he tell the guests, 'Okay, everyone, gather round, let me tell you all about my inventory problems.' No, he had faith that it would all work out."

"No," I said, "what he *had* was Jesus as a wedding guest."

"Exactly, and Jesus was quietly informed about the problem. It was all done discreetly, everyone had a good time, everything worked out."

"You've lost me." I sighed. "Are you proposing that we put this commercial on the air, take their money, and then expect Jesus to do the rest? And when the customers call to complain, they get a recorded announcement: 'For information regarding the status of your wine, please contact Jesus directly—and be sure to refer to your eight-digit order number. God bless and have a nice day!' "

"All I'm suggesting is that we worry about selling first, and supplying later. For now, let's trust in God to provide the wine when we need it."

Philomena fixed her hazel eyes on me. I was unable to argue with her. At that moment, her interpretation of the story in my breviary seemed somehow to make perfect sense. She had revealed to me the Third Law of Spiritual and Financial Growth:

III.

AS LONG AS GOD KNOWS THE TRUTH, IT DOESN'T MATTER WHAT YOU TELL YOUR CUSTOMERS.

Market Meditation
the Third

Who's more important, anyway—God or my customers?
Have I ever profited by lying to a customer? (Be honest, now!)
Did God know I was lying?
Did He stop the sale?
Is it just possible that God is a salesman too?
Am I on God's sales force?
Okay now, does God want me to
(a) tell the truth, or (b) help the team meet its sales target?

Your questions show that you're really beginning to "get" the meaning of Cana. Now, to deepen your understanding, take out that calculator and a piece of paper. Let's consider: What kind of wine were they serving at Cana? White or red? If in A.D. 30 a firkin of decent wine, the kind you'd serve at your daughter's wedding, cost .42 shekels, how much, in today's dollars, did the host save by inviting Jesus to the wedding feast? (Don't forget to factor in what it cost to feed the disciples!) For extra credit, what is a firkin?

After Cana, do you suppose Jesus got invited to a lot of weddings?

Prayer of
the Mendacious Salesman

Almighty God, Top Salesman of the Universe,
Master of Pitches and Presentations,
grant that I should exceed my quota, and that the truth
shall not stay my tongue from its appointed task.
Grant, too, that the customer will not learn of my inventory
problem until after his credit-card number
has been obtained, so that when the sale is celebrated, my glass,
and Thine, shall overflow with wine as crisp, full-bodied,
and attractively priced as that which Thou, in Thy Infinite
Hospitality, served that day at Cana in Galilee.

CHAPTER THE FOURTH

In Vino Veritas…
A Surprise Visitor…
A Sermon on a Mount

HILOMENA MANAGED TO place the Cana commercial at just the right moment in *The Sound of Music:* immediately following the wedding scene. We watched along with thirty million other Americans as Julie Andrews plighted her troth to Christopher Plummer. The audience at Saint Thad's cheered for our fellow religious when the camera showed the nuns peering out at the ceremony from their cloister. Then we cheered at our commercial.

Seconds after the screen showed 800-TRY-CANA our phones began ringing like church bells after High Mass on

Easter Sunday. Philomena had set up our phone bank and trained the monks. Dozens of monks sat at their cubicles, wearing operator headsets and saying to every caller, "God bless you—may I take your order?" The Abbot had wanted to include a Chopran "Thank you for going first-class," but Philomena had managed to veto it on the grounds that it didn't sound very monastic.

It was all we could do to keep up. Over the next several weeks, we received orders for a million bottles of Cana wine at eight dollars a bottle. The commercial had charmed not only the viewers but also the press. Reporters from the national media began to turn up on our doorstep. They were somewhat disappointed to find, in lieu of an alpine fortress-monastery, a squat brick affair without drawbridge or snowcapped peak looming above. As he gave them tours of the facilities, the Abbot began referring to the nearby hillock as Mount Cana. (He neglected to mention that it was in fact a mound of garbage. During the days of tribulation, the monastery had leased the land to a waste-disposal operator for use as a dump.) But having come all this way, the reporters and producers were not about to let the facts get in the way of a heartwarming story. Their camera crews used creative angles to make Cana look as formidable as possible; by shooting from ground level, they even managed to make the hillock loom large, if not like an alp, with the Abbot climbing it à la Julie Andrews.

One day while he was giving Diane Sawyer of ABC a tour of the wine-making facility, the Abbot got so carried away that he offered her a taste of the new batch. Philomena clutched my arm in a death grip and whispered, "If Diane

Sawyer spits up our wine on prime-time television, we're going to have an image problem, big-time." Before the Abbot could uncork the bottle, which had the trademark Cana orangy tinge, Philomena stepped forward.

"Now, Father," she said smoothly, "remember how you're always telling us that you'll serve no wine 'before it's divine'? Shouldn't we offer Ms. Sawyer something from the Abbot's Own Reserve?"

"Allow me," I interjected. I ran off to the Abbot's office and rummaged through the cases of French wine he had ordered—"for R&D purposes," as he put it. I grabbed a bottle of some 1982 French wine called Château Figeac and quickly poured it into an empty bottle labeled "Abbot's Own," spilling a good deal of it in the process. I jammed the cork halfway back in, and hurried back.

Ms. Sawyer sipped for the cameras. "Wow!" she exclaimed. "I'd heard New York State wine was getting good, but I had no *idea*. How do you do it?"

"Well," the Abbot said, "much as the Lord loves the cheerful giver, we can't give away Cana's secrets. After all, Jesus didn't explain His secret at the wedding feast of Cana, did He?"

My eyes strayed to the cork, which the Abbot was holding in his hand. To my horror, I saw the words CHÂTEAU FIGEAC clearly stamped on it. But Ms. Sawyer concluded the interview without noticing it, for which I offered up a silent prayer of thanksgiving.

Afterward, the Abbot congratulated me on my intervention. On the way back to his office, he said, "That was a Figeac, wasn't it?"

I nodded.

"Smooth as silk, hints of blackberry and pistachio. Lovely finish. Must have been the '82."

"I see Father Abbot's R&D is paying off," I said. "So how much does a bottle of Château Figeac '82 go for?"

"More than a bottle of Cana '82, I can tell you. That's *if* you can find it. But I know someone in Chicago who has a few bottles left for under two hundred apiece. He even has some of the '61."

Back in his office, the Abbot frowned when he saw the puddle of spilled Figeac on the linoleum floor. "That's what I call a sin." He poured what remained in the bottle into a glass and handed it to Philomena.

"Delicious," she said. "That was an admirable feat of wine stewardship, Brother Ty."

"Thank you," I replied, "but I'm not sure it's a viable long-term strategy. We have orders for one million bottles. If we go on putting two-hundred-dollar wine into bottles we sell for eight bucks"—I reached for the Abbot's calculator—"our net profit will be . . . minus $192 million. You're the one with the MBA, but to me this does not sound like a dazzling business plan."

A horrified look came over the Abbot. "Give my Figeac away to people looking for an eight-dollar wine? *Numquam!*"[16]

"Of course not," Philomena smiled coyly at the Abbot. "You're saving the best for *thee*."

The two of them chuckled in a way I found irritating.

---

[16] Latin: "Never."

"Then what," I said, "*are* we planning to serve our wedding guests?"

"The Chilean wine," said the Abbot. "The wine you were going to get when you were rerouted by Brother Deepak."

Not this again. "You mean when Our Heavenly Broker passed on the tip about Apple?"

Philomena intervened to avert fierce theological debate. "It can't be all Chilean wine," she said. "The marketing appeal of Cana is that it's grown, trampled, and bottled here by monks. If the label is going to say 'Produced at the Monastery of Cana,' then legally speaking, we've got to make it here."

"Exactly," I said, "which means we need new equipment to make wine. Our own wine. Wine that is free of rust. Wine that is not orange."

"Details," the Abbot said with disdain. "We'll bottle the Chilean wine here, add a little of our own—but not so much that we'd ruin the taste."

"All right, but we *still need new equipment*," I said. "We've processed the credit-card orders for one million bottles of wine. We now have to produce one million bottles. Of *something*."

The Abbot grudgingly agreed to provide funds for new wine-bottling equipment, although he seemed to have lost interest in any domestically produced wine. His mind these days was on other projects. Construction was under way on his executive suite, and now, ominously, he had seized on an even more ambitious plan.

As a result of the media coverage, dozens of visitors a week were turning up on our doorstep, asking to see the winery and, of course, the snowcapped "Mount Cana."

Brother Jerome, newly appointed Director of Pilgrim Relations, managed effectively to befuddle them. The Abbot, meanwhile, had discerned a potential new income stream in the visitors. He and Elliott drew up plans for a real-life Mount Cana. "If they're coming," the Abbot observed, "we might as well build it."

THE FIRST ANGRY letters began to arrive. It had been months since the commercial, and customers were wondering where their wine was. The Abbot, consumed with office renovation and mountain-making, appointed me Director of Fulfillment. It fell to me to explain to the disgruntled multitude that "our humble operation" had been "overwhelmed by popular demand," but that the monks were working around the clock to fill the orders. Ironically, my lame prevarications had a salutary effect. Once word got out that Cana was unobtainable, even more orders flooded in. Philomena promptly raised the price from eight dollars to fifteen dollars a bottle. I was now able to tell the complaining customers that at least they had gotten in "on the ground floor." The Abbot began talking about selling Cana wine futures.

One morning Brother Jerome brought me a visitor. "I gave him the tour," he whispered. "I even showed him my pigs. But he has some kind of badge. He says he wants to see the person in charge of the winery."

He did have a badge, and it said BUREAU OF ALCOHOL, TOBACCO AND FIREARMS.

"I don't suppose," I said, trying to sound casual, "that you're here about tobacco or firearms."

It was quickly clear he was not one for banter. The BATF had been receiving complaints from customers and the attorneys general of several states about the unfulfilled orders. He was here to investigate. I explained about the huge volume of orders. He took notes about the orders, quizzing me about our acreage and capacity. He asked why no wine was flowing through our shiny new equipment.

"Ah," I said, "you should really talk to the Abbot about that." We found the Abbot conferring with Elliott and the theme-park architect brought in to work on Mount Cana. The Abbot greeted the federal agent graciously, to the point of offering him a glass of wine.

"I haven't seen any wine so far," the agent said.

"Ahh," the Abbot said. "Well, you should really talk to Brother Ty here about that. He is our Director of Fulfillment."

"Why don't you both talk to me about it," the agent said. He pointed out the obvious, that we didn't grow nearly enough grapes to fill all the orders, and that we weren't producing anything at the moment. Then he pointed out something not obvious.

"That TV interview you did with Diane Sawyer. One of our guys—he knows his wines—took a close look at the video tape where she's tasting your wine. He made out the word 'Figeac' on the cork."

"Ahhh," the Abbot said. "Well, the way things are going, Cana may soon cost as much as Figeac."

"That's not the point," the agent said. "It's against federal law to pass one wine off for another."

The Abbot drew himself up. " 'Render unto Caesar the things which are Caesar's, and unto God that are God's.' We will respect the laws of the land. Meanwhile, I suggest that you respect the laws of God. We are a humble order—"

Unfortunately, the Abbot's sentence was interrupted by the sound of a bulldozer gouging earth for his new wine cellar. The agent made a pointed remark about the extensive work, and the conversation deteriorated. It ended with the Abbot reminding the agent that there were "a hundred million taxpaying Catholics" in America.

"I wonder how they'll feel when they learn that their tax dollars are being used to persecute Mother Church," the Abbot said. "I'm sure Diane would be interested in a follow-up piece. 'Big Brother Beats Up Little Brothers.' "

Diane?

I got the agent away from the Abbot and did what I could to soothe him. I promised him that the orders would be fulfilled soon, using our own wine blended with other wines, and that the labels would be in strict accordance with all the regulations.

As soon as I had shown the BATF agent to the door, I rushed back to the Abbot. He blandly reassured me that the Chilean wine had been ordered "weeks ago," and resumed his discussion about the fake mountain with Elliott and the theme-park designer.

I called the manager of the winery in the Maipo Valley to inquire when the wine would arrive. My Spanish was rusty, but good enough to make out that the "*cheque*"[17] the Abbot had sent them for $1.5 million had turned out to be "*mal*."[18] I

---

[17] Check.
[18] Bad—that is, bounced.

gathered further that they had notified the Abbot and that he had told them it was all a misunderstanding and that another one would be on its way. Yet no *cheque* had arrived.

Sensing a catastrophe looming, I called the bank to find out how much we had in our account. The answer was $36,000. No wonder the $1.5 million check to the Chilean winery had bounced. At the rate the Abbot was spending money—on his suite, on his wine cellar, and now on an ersatz alp—that would last about a week. But if we didn't start to fulfill those orders for Cana wine soon, that BATF agent would be back, bearing unpleasant legal papers.

It was no use trying to persuade the Abbot to focus on this emergency. He brushed me off with Chopran platitudes about the universe finding a way. I did, however, get Philomena's attention. Together we went over the Abbot's building budgets—Elliott's bills were merely astronomical, whereas the theme-park designer's could be described as "alarming"—and the costs of filling the wine orders. By the end, we had determined that we needed $5 million, and we needed it quickly.

I decided to tap our account at Wall Street. Using tips that Our Lord, in His wisdom and infinite generosity, had seen fit to bestow on me through my readings of the breviary, my Cana Fund had grown very nicely and done well for other clients of Bill who had invested in it. Bill told me, in fact, that the Cana Fund's performance, along with my successful pork bellies and Apple tips, had made me into something of a guru down at the old firm. He said they thought I had "connections." If only they knew.

I called Bill and asked him how much equity we had in the fund. "Just over a mil," he said; not nearly enough to rescue us.

That night I paced restlessly in the cloister. The evening's reading in the breviary was a familiar one, from the gospel of Mark 10:25: "It is easier for a camel to go through the eye of a needle than for a rich man to enter into the kingdom of heaven." It was a tart bit of wisdom considering our predicament. At first I thought it was a reproachful message from God, a reminder that the riches bestowed on the monastery were hindering our spiritual development. Then it struck me: Our Broker was on the phone again, telling me how to save the monastery—and a few rich men's souls to boot.

MY ARRIVAL AT the firm, wearing monastic habit, caused a stir. Heads looked up and turned as I walked past the trading floor toward Bill's office. Old friends rushed up to shake my hand, and even those with whom I had not particularly gotten along greeted me respectfully.

"Hey, Father!" one called out. "What's hot?"

"Hell," I replied. "And that's the only tip you sinners will get from me today." I made sure to walk past Jerry's desk. Jerry was notorious in the firm for stealing other brokers' hot tips. In the old days he had pretty much ignored me—no one wanted to steal *my* information. The only time he paid any attention to me was when he taunted me for my drinking.

He saw me, all right. But then you would have to be blind not to notice a monk on a Wall Street trading floor. I said to Bill, loudly enough for Jerry to overhear, "I need to talk to you in *private.*"

I had picked the lunch hour so that Jerry could follow us out without being noticeable. On the elevator down, I even complimented him on his (ghastly) necktie.

I had asked Slattery to save two adjacent booths. Bill and I sat down in one. A moment later Jerry slipped into the one that "happened" to be free next to us, and pretended to immerse himself in his *Wall Street Journal*.

Again in a voice loud enough to be overheard, I said, "Bill, you know the story in the Bible about how it is easier for a camel to go through the eye of a needle than for a rich man to enter the kingdom of heaven?"

He looked suspicious. "You didn't get me down here to . . . you're not trying to recruit me into your order?"

"It would take a Second Coming to do that. Nothing of the sort. Just listen. Suppose that needle were attached to a Singer sewing machine?"

"What are you talking about?"

"Camel?" I prompted him. "Needle?"

"I still don't know what you're talking about."

"I'm talking about one corporation acquiring another corporation."

His face changed from incomprehension to astonishment. "You mean . . . RJR is about to buy Singer?"

"Other way around. RJR is about to be bought by Singer Sewing Machine."

"Jesus," he whispered.

"You did not hear this from me. Now, I want one million in RJR calls. Right away. This is happening even as we speak."

Bill whipped out his cell phone. "No," I said, touching his wrist, "do it on a hard line. The pay phone."

Bill went to the pay phone by the bar. I stood up and pretended to notice Jerry for the first time. He had already taken out *his* cell phone.

"Jerry!" I said. "I didn't see you. Will you join us?"

Jerry looked stricken. "Uh, no, actually, whoops, look at the time. Gotta run."

"But you haven't eaten."

"Just remembered, gotta call a client."

I pointed to his cell phone. "Go ahead and call him."

"Battery's dead." I continued to torment him with diversionary small talk. His face took on a martyred look when I began a lengthy analysis of the recent weather, a subject no one on Wall Street discusses unless it affects crop prices. Finally he could take no more.

"Gotta make that call," he said as he shot out of the booth like a greyhound at the racetrack.

Bill returned from his phone call.

"Done," he said. "I bought myself some, too, on the side."

"Listen to me very carefully, Bill. When my options are worth five million, I want you to pull me out. Have you got that?" He looked puzzled. After all, why pull out when the stock is still rising? I said emphatically, "Just do it. And pull yourself out, too."

I made him swear. Though I wanted Bill to get into heaven, I didn't want to ruin him in the process.

Within the hour the word was out on the Street that RJR, the tobacco giant, was in play. That afternoon its stock shot up eight points. By 3:40 P.M., minutes before the closing bell, my call options were worth five and a half million dollars.

I called Bill. "Have you sold them?"

He said that it had been no problem selling them at all.

"Did you sell yours?" I caught a note of hesitation. *"Bill?"*

He promised me he would sell his.

The next morning RJR and Singer announced that there was no takeover planned, hostile or friendly. RJR's stock dropped back to where it had been.

As I was driving back to Cana, Bill reached me on my cell phone to say that Jerry had gone down "in flames." I rebuked myself for feeling so happy to hear that, but reasoned that while I had made Jerry's life on earth hell, I had made it easier for him to enter heaven.

THE MONEY FLOWED from our account to Chile, and soon Maipo Valley cabernet was flowing through our new equipment. We assembled on a balmy summer evening to watch the first bottle of Cana Abbot's Own be filled. Just before it reached the automatic corker, it passed by Brother Theo. In his new capacity as Master Blender, he stood over the conveyor with an eyedropper filled with wine produced from our own grapes. As each bottle went by, he squeezed a drop into the neck. It was the Abbot's judgment that this minuscule amount of our own wretched wine legally justified the label's "Produced by the monks of the Monastery of Cana." This was not a legal opinion I wanted to run by the Bureau of Alcohol, Tobacco and Firearms.

The Abbot poured the first glass for himself as we all watched. He held it up to the light, swirled it around, sniffed, and then sipped. I thought I saw him wince at this low-budget wine, but then his taste had, as he put it, "matured." But he smiled and pronounced it "eminently drinkable."

He made a gracious speech complimenting all the monks for making it through our time of tribulation. He made a toast

to "our phenomenal Philomena" for "her miraculous intervention at Cana," and poured her the second glass. Philomena
raised the glass, thanked him, and then turned to me.

"If anyone pulled off a miracle at Cana," she said, "it was
Brother Ty." She handed me the glass.

She had no idea of my past trouble with drinking. It had
been almost three years now since alcohol had passed my
lips that day at Slattery's. But this was no time to go into all
that. It would have seemed churlish to turn down one cele-
bratory glass of wine. Besides, I was curious about this wine
that had taken such effort to obtain. What—finally—did it
taste like?

The answer was, eminently drinkable. I would have felt
better if our customers were paying six dollars a bottle for it
instead of the fifteen dollars we were now charging. But it
was free of rust particles and orangy hues. In fact, it wasn't
bad at all. As we sat down to the outdoor feast the Abbot had
arranged for the occasion, I allowed myself another glass.

We had never feasted like this. Elliott had hired a caterer
from New York City. At each place setting was an illuminated menu in the style of the medieval manuscripts pains-
takingly illustrated by monks. As the wine warmed my
innards, I studied the elegant calligraphy:

"A Feast at Cana"

CHEF PATRICK O'NEILL'S MODERN INTERPRETATION
OF A GALILEAN WEDDING BANQUET

Mound of Olives

Dead Sea Rolls

Manna-cotti

Pork Loin Gadarene stuffed with Amaretto figs

Poached Monkfish in parchment

Fallen Angelcake Magdalene

Café Lazarus

Firkins of "Abbot's Own" Cana Cabernet

In the center of the head table, where the Abbot and
Philomena were seated—for some reason, I had not been included—was an enormous ice sculpture depicting the new
Mount Cana complex, including the Abbot's latest vision, a
huge Pilgrims Center.

"At the original feast of Cana," said Brother Bob, poking
at his pork loin Gadarene, "they must have had a hard time
keeping the ice sculpture from melting. Or did the Blessed
Mother ask Jesus to fix that, too?"

I was concentrating more on the scene next to the sculpture. The Abbot was in high spirits, pouring himself and
Philomena glass after glass—from a bottle that looked familiar. Even in the fading light I could make out the word
"Figeac" on the label. They were talking intently. The Abbot
occasionally touched her elbow or sleeve to emphasize a
point—no doubt some timeless theological gem from the
Chopran canon they shared. When at one point he put his
entire arm around her shoulder, it was more than I could
stand. I grabbed a firkin of Cana from our table and stalked
off into the vineyard.

I climbed Mount Cana—that is, the original "Mount Cana," the hillock over the old garbage dump—and listened to the sounds of the feast below. The moon rose behind the skeleton of the new Mount Cana. How ridiculous it looked: steel girders welded together to make a fifteen-story-high alp. What had become of our monastery?

More to the point, what had become of me? Here I was, sitting on a garbage dump drinking bogus wine, consumed with jealousy over my religious superior. In my inebriated fog, I tried to imagine what kind of mortification Saint Thad would prescribe for this spiritual state. A lot more than a roll in the brambles. I drained the firkin and hurled it at the new Mount Cana. Then I lay back and experienced an old and familiar sensation—passing out.

The next thing I recall was a voice. "Ty? Are you all right?" It was Philomena, standing over me, the moon shining above her like a halo. Two halos, actually. I blinked, trying to uncross my eyes.

"Saint Philomena," I muttered.

"Brother Bob told me you'd stomped off with a bottle. I'm sorry," she said. "If I'd known about your...I wouldn't have offered you that glass of wine."

"I only wish it had been Figeac," I said. "But I suppose that's just for your intimate moments with my spiritual leader."

"If you weren't so drunk," she said, "I'd take offense at that."

"Hunh," I quipped.

"*Ty*. If you suspect the Abbot of impure thoughts, that's your business. But I can assure you that they're not reciprocated by me."

"Then I guess it's just a spiritual thing between you two Chopraheads."

"Chopra? What are you talking about?"

"You met at a Choprahead convention, didn't you?"

She laughed incredulously. "Yes. My firm sent me there to drum up business. You don't think I take those books seriously, do you? I admire the guy's marketing savvy, but I wouldn't read his books on my own time."

So that was it. My respect for Philomena soared. I patted the dewy grass beside me and said, "Pull up a seat." She sat down.

"Okay," I said, "so you don't believe in Deepak. You don't believe in selling honestly labeled wine. What *do* you believe in?"

"It may come as a shock to you," she said, "but I believe in the Catholic thing."

"The Catholic *thing*?" I said. "I don't think we covered that in Church Dogma 101. Does 'the Catholic thing' include exploiting Holy Scripture for fraudulent commercial purposes? Do you really believe that God wants us to get rich quick off His miracle? Do you even believe there *was* a miracle at Cana?"

"Well, Your Holiness," she replied, "it so happens that I've done some reading on the matter. I don't make a commercial without doing my homework. And what I learned about Cana is that—maybe He did, and maybe He didn't. The story appears only in the Gospel of John, and John is considered by theologians to be the least reliable of the four. The other three don't mention it at all. Bottom line? Maybe it doesn't matter whether He did it or didn't. What matters is that people believe He did."

"I get it. John the Evangelist—marketing consultant."

"As a matter of fact, yeah. How do you think the Catholic faith spread around the world? Brilliant marketing."

"Why do you have to be so cynical?"

"It's easy if your name is Philomena."

"Why?" I replied. "It's a lovely name. It means 'beloved.' Doesn't it?"

"In 1802 they found a skeleton of a young woman in the Roman catacombs. They decided it was the body of an early virgin martyr named Philomena. The relic was given to a church in Naples. Pilgrims came flocking to the Church— with donations. Then a hundred years later they decide they're not Philomena's bones after all. They don't know whose bones they are. Maybe she wasn't a martyr. Or a virgin. So the Church declares her a nonsaint. The cult goes ballistic, especially the priests at all the churches around the world named Saint Philomena. So Pope Paul VI says, Okay, go on praying to her."

"And keep those donations coming," I added. Philomena laughed.

"Yeah, I'm a little cynical. When you're named after 'Saint' Philomena, you're entitled to a little skepticism. So, Your Holiness, you can sit there like the Defender of the Faith denouncing my commercial as blasphemy, but it's doing the same thing as those bones of that teenaged girl— making money for a good cause."

"By 'good cause' do you mean the Abbot's wine cellar? Or"—I gestured at the moonlit skeleton—"Mount Cana?"

"I'm not saying money isn't corrupting. The Abbot's wine cellar isn't the first perk in the history of the Catholic Church. Have you been to the Vatican lately?"

She looked beautiful, sitting there in the wet grass. I had no more appetite for theological debate. The only thing I wanted to know at this point was what happened next in that scene from *The Thorn Birds*. The day after Philomena had read us the passage, I'd gone to the bookstore to buy a copy. The moment I walked in, the clerk said to me, "Let me guess, *The Thorn Birds*. Sorry, but we're plumb out." He explained that I was the fourteenth monk that day to come in looking for it.

"Philomena," I said, "can I ask a completely nontheological question? It's been weighing on me."

"Yes," she said.

"What happens next in that scene from *The Thorn Birds?* The one where Meggie puts her arm around the priest?"

Philomena smiled. "It's funny you mentioned that."

"Why?"

"I was just thinking that in this moonlight you look a little like Richard Chamberlain."[19]

"Oh," I said.

She giggled. So she was a bit tipsy herself. "Can I ask you a question?"

"All right."

"When you were on the outside, on Wall Street, did you ever come close to getting married? Or weren't you ..."

"I'm not gay, if that's what you mean. I dated, but somehow things just never ... I don't know ..."

"Worked out? I know."

---

[19] The actor who played Father (later Cardinal) Ralph de Bricassart in the TV miniseries of *The Thorn Birds*.

We sat there a bit awkwardly in the moonlight.

"So you want to know what happens next?" Philomena asked.

I nodded. She put her arm around my neck and kissed me.

✠

THE FEAST WAS winding down by the time we walked back into the courtyard. Fortunately, the remaining monks were in no condition to notice our walking in together. One of Brother Jerome's pigs had gotten loose and was rooting through what looked like the remains of the Fallen Magdalene cake. Brother Algernon was slumped over the table, snoring. The ice sculpture of Mount Cana had created an icy puddle that was dripping onto the prone figure of Brother Tom. Brother Jerome, oblivious to his loose pig, was wearing his new Walkman, bobbing and weaving. As we passed him we could hear the sound coming from his earphones, "Staying alive!... Staying alive!"

I tapped him on the shoulder to tell him about his pig.

"WHAT!" he screamed. I motioned to him to take off his earphones.

"Your pig," I said.

"*You're* a pig!"—he giggled.

"No. Your *pig*." I pointed to the animal. "It's loose. You better do something before it starts to eat Brother Tom."

"Great party," he said. "It is nice that we're doing so well now, isn't it?"

"That's the spirit," said Philomena. "I've been trying to tell Brother Ty he shouldn't feel guilty about our good fortune."

"Yes," he said, "we've worked hard, and this is our reward." He put his earphones back on and walked off to cor-
ral his pig. He stopped and turned around. He grinned at us
and shouted over the Bee Gees a line I would never forget.
It was, I realized later, the Fourth Law of Spiritual and Financial Growth:

IV.

MONEY IS GOD'S WAY OF SAYING "THANKS!"

Market Meditation
the Fourth

How many times have I actually seen a camel
not fit through the eye of a needle?
How many times have I seen a rich man
not enter the kingdom of heaven?
If God didn't want anyone to be rich,
why did He make so much money?
"Manna" sounds an awful lot like "money,"
doesn't it? How about "moola"?
Doesn't a good sales manager give his best employees a bonus?
Isn't God a good sales manager?
If someone gave me a nice present,
would it be polite to hurl it back in his face?
Should I do that to God?
Is insulting God going to make it any easier
for me to enter the kingdom of heaven?

Excellent questions! Take a piece of paper. Draw a vertical line down the middle. On the left side, make a list of all the nice things you own. On the right side, write down exactly how you got each of them. (E.g., next to 35-inch TV: "I put it on my MasterCard"[20])

See a pattern developing in the second column? How did you get them? For every single item *you had to pay money*!

Now, turn the sheet of paper over and write down every-

---

[20] It's okay if you can't remember exactly which card you used. God knows.

thing that you don't have that you want. (E.g., "42-inch TV"[21]) Okay: how are you going to get all these things? That's right. *More money!*

And where is that money going to come from? Where do all good things come from? That's right. God.

Now take the piece of paper. Fold it once lengthwise. Then fold the ends back so that they form triangles. Refold the triangles. Refold them again. Is it beginning to look like a "paper airplane"?

Now write down on the left wing how much more money you want. On the right wing, write down how much money you're willing to settle for. Ready to launch? Hold the airmail between your fingers, go to the nearest window and open it. Ready? Let 'er rip![22]

Now—*very important*—as you sit back and wait for God to send some "paper" back your way, ask yourself: When God says, "Thanks," how do I say, "You're welcome!"?

Hint: see next chapter.

---

[21] You don't have to specify which brand.
[22] If you're doing this in the office, do not break the window to open it. Go to the roof or the parking lot.

Prayer of Untroubled Wealth

O Lord, Supreme Rewarder and Bestower of Bonuses,
whose incentive package led Thy people
through the wilderness, grant that when Thou showereth
me with money that I have the strength to grasp it,
the serenity to accept it without guilt, and the wisdom to
recognize that this is Thy way of expressing gratitude.

CHAPTER THE FIFTH

The Vatican Is Vexed…
The Abbot Is Miffed…
A Game of Biblical Chess

IT WAS A VERY GOOD YEAR. During the twelve months after the first bottle came off the line, we produced more than six million bottles of Abbot's Own (none of which I drank, fortunately). Trucks arrived regularly with containers of Chilean wine, and Brother Theo's eyedropper operation had to be automated. We cleared over $25 million in profits from the wine alone. Meanwhile my Cana Fund was flourishing. A computer consultant helped me put the breviary into a database called BREVNET that compared our daily readings with mar-

ket developments around the world. Even more money
began gushing in when the new Mount Cana Pilgrims Center opened. Brent's new Cana commercials drew bigger
crowds, and Philomena was ready for them. To my delight
she had accepted our offer to become Director for Pilgrim
Development, and had taken up residence in a spacious
apartment over the Center.

Then one midsummer morning, our community's tran-
quillity was shattered by an unexpected visitor from Rome.

We were in the Abbot's now finished executive suite with
Elliott and the theme-park designer, discussing the Abbot's
notion of adding a "wine slide" to Mount Cana. They had
come with the model. As Elliott explained, "They have to
earn the ride. Everybody gets a staff to help them make their
little pilgrimage up the mountain. We've put a little shrine
along the way to inspire them, Saint Thad in the brambles.
There's a little box if they want to make a donation. Nice.
Then they get to the top, where they get their reward. The
first thing they see is this *immense* firkin—I love that word
and I *still* don't know what it means. A mechanical servant is
pouring clear water into it, and dark red water—the wine—
is flowing out, from a different circulating system, because
of course we're not really changing water into wine here.
They get into these four-seater boats, fabulous, in the shape
of wine casks cut in half. And they're off. They get to the waterfall and *whoosh* down the slide. There'll be a sign telling
Mom not to worry, this red 'wine' doesn't stain."

Philomena and I exchanged worried glances. "It's very
nice, Elliott," she said, "but I'm worried about our image. We
have to protect the Cana franchise."

"How many pilgrims per hour can it handle?" the Abbot asked.

At that moment we were interrupted by Brother Mike, an efficient young monk who had recently joined Cana and become the Abbot's executive assistant. He came into the room and handed the Abbot a business card.

"He's waiting in the reception area."

The Abbot stared at the card. He read aloud, "Monsignor Raffaello Maraviglia...Segretario Esecutivo...Ufficio dell' Investigazione Interna...Vaticano...Vatican internal investigation?" Suddenly he paled. "Good God, that's Cardinal Blutschpiller's office!"

Cana was a long way from the Vatican, but even we humble monks knew the reputation of Franz Cardinal Blutschpiller. He was the most feared man in the Church. He was called "The Great Excommunicator"—the Pope's personal enforcer. And now his executive secretary was standing in our reception area.

The Abbot ran off to greet him. A minute later the door opened and we heard the Abbot saying, "Now, this is our new Executive Retreat Center..."

The man who entered was in his forties, tall and lean with high cheekbones, cobalt eyes, and a cleft chin. He was wearing a beautifully tailored black suit over a monsignor's purple vest and a large silver crucifix on a chain.

Philomena stared. I didn't have to ask why. He bore an uncanny resemblance to Richard Chamberlain. Elliott was transfixed, too, perhaps by the suit.

The Abbot introduced us. Monsignor Maraviglia[23] had a

---

[23] The "g" is silent.

gracious but somewhat distant manner. There was an awkward moment when the Monsignor addressed Elliott as "Brother."

"I wear black," Elliott explained, "but I'm not with the order."

The Monsignor's eyes flicked about the room while we made chitchat about Cardinal Blutschpiller's health, in particular his recent prostate operation. As the Abbot began expounding on the upstate New York weather and its impact on local viticulture, the Monsignor's cold blue eyes settled on the model. He leaned over and examined the figurines in casks going over the waterfall. He studied the miniature sign over the entrance arch.

" 'Cana Cask-Ade'..." he read. He seemed puzzled, but then smiled thinly. "Of course, *cascata*. Waterfall, wine casks. A pun."

"A joke of our friend, here," said the Abbot, in Elliott's direction. "He brought this in. Isn't it...funny?"

"Most unusual," said Monsignor Maraviglia. "So you're planning to add this to your mountain?"

"We thought it would be a way of bringing Scripture to life," the Abbot said. "While cooling the pilgrims down. It can get quite hot here, summers. So, what brings you to Cana?"

"We've heard much about you," the Monsignor said. "I have seen your commercial."

"Oh," said the Abbot, "you must talk to Brother Ty and Philomena here about that. That was their project."

"Most impressive." He smiled at Philomena. It was the first hint of warmth I detected. Philomena blushed.

He turned to the Abbot and said, "His Eminence the Cardinal has asked me to come here to study your methods."

"Ah," the Abbot said.

The Monsignor clapped his hands together. "Well, a tour?"

The Abbot said, "Surely Monsignor is exhausted after his journey? A nap…"

"I slept at the motel in town last night. I wanted to get an early start."

"Oh. Well then, where shall we begin…"

"Why not here." The Monsignor's eyes made a damning sweep of the room's opulence. "This is your 'Executive Retreat Center'?"

"Yes," said the Abbot. "For visiting executives. Of course, they expect a certain level of comfort."

"Naturally." The Monsignor strolled to the atrium with the four alabaster columns and the marble Etruscan fountain.

The Abbot began explaining how running water is conducive to contemplation, but the Monsignor was already moving toward the multimedia room. He sat down on the Italian leather sofa.

"Very comfortable," he said. "And that…" He pointed to the large screen on the wall.

"This is where we show them films," said the Abbot. "Inspirational films. Documentaries…"

The Monsignor was on the move again, heading down the stairs to the wine cellar. A look of alarm came over the Abbot's face. The Monsignor was gone for a good five minutes.

"An excellent cellar," he said upon emerging. "Though I didn't see any bottles of your own wine." He moved on to the adjoining bedchamber. "And this?"

"A guest bedroom, for retreatants."

The room had a distinctly lived-in look. Monastic clothing was strewn about. The down comforter on the bed was rumpled. The TV at the foot of the bed was piled with Deepak Chopra videos on weight loss and spirituality. On the nightstand was a bottle of half-drunk Bordeaux (Duhart-Milon Rothschild '76), a large bottle of aspirin, *TV Guide*, and a stack of jazz CDs. "Someone is staying here?"

"Not at the moment," said the Abbot. "I sometimes use it during the day. For contemplation...a quick restorative... nap. Of course I have a cell, just like the other monks."

Monsignor Maraviglia nodded. "Yes, of course. Well, let's see the rest of this...monastery."

The Abbot reluctantly led the way to the cells. Music emanated from some. As we walked past Brother Ed's I thought I detected the theme music to *Baywatch*. The Monsignor moved along impassively, until we heard rather loud snoring coming from Brother Tom's cell. The Monsignor glanced at his wristwatch. "Is it ten-fifteen your time?"

The Abbot nodded grimly. Then he tried, "Since we rise so early, we instituted a 'little hour,' for private contemplation. You know...reflection."

"Very important," said Maraviglia. "And your cell?"

"Just down the hall."

The door to the Abbot's old cell opened with a creak. Everything was covered with a layer of undisturbed dust. The nightlamp was latticed with cobwebs. On the metal bed frame was a bare mattress.

"You set a good example for the other monks," said the Monsignor. "Doesn't Saint Thaddeus inveigh against blankets in *De Doloribus Extremis*? Book Eight, no? 'Let thy bed be as rock, and cover thy body only with coarse hay and thorns.' "

"Why don't we move on to the Pilgrims Center," suggested the Abbot.

Philomena took the Monsignor through the wine-tasting room, the feasting room—the sign said NEXT FEAST: 12 PM—the wedding chapel and the gift shop, with its Mount Cana key rings and monk-shaped decanters. It was the first time I had seen Philomena embarrassed by her marketing creations. The Monsignor was unfailingly gracious, even when he saw the T-shirt with the picture of the wine jug on the front and this on the back:

MY PARENTS WENT
TO MOUNT CANA
AND ALL THEY GOT ME
WAS THIS FIRKIN T-SHIRT

"It's a way of teaching them weights and measures of the Bible," Philomena said. "A firkin would be—"

"Thirty-six liters," he said.

We returned to the Executive Retreat Center.

"So," said the Abbot over coffee—wisely, not from his personal espresso machine—"how long can you stay?"

"From what I have seen," the Monsignor said, stirring his coffee thoughtfully, "my study will take some time. I wish to be very careful. And fair. We would not want mistaken impressions to be formed. Or made public."

"Certainly not," said the Abbot, helpless to protest. Not only was the Monsignor the Abbot's religious superior, but he also had the power to ruin forever the Cana brand name.

"Anything we can do to assist. Brother Ty has a financial background. He knows our operations intimately. He'll help you in any way."

"Thank you. I will call on Brother Ty. But, Philomena, did you mention that you have a degree in business administration?"

Philomena nodded.

"Then perhaps if you could be my guide?" He turned to the Abbot. "If you can spare her?"

"A guide," the Abbot said. "Of course. Anything to help His Eminence."

Maraviglia asked, "Do you have any retreats scheduled?"

"Not—in the immediate future. That I can think of . . ."

"Then perhaps I could stay here."

"Here?"

The Monsignor pointed. "The guest bedroom."

"Ah," the Abbot said. He looked stricken. "Well, if . . . you think you'll be content with our poor hospitality."

The Monsignor smiled, " 'Take whatever is given to you, and bear thy suffering in silence and with cheer.' *De Doloribus,* Book Four."

THE NEXT MORNING all the monks assembled in chapel for Matins promptly at 5:00 A.M., for the first time in a while. Attendance had been dwindling since the Abbot, citing the "evolving nature of Cana's mission," had relaxed monastic routine and instituted a policy of *in camera*[24] prayer. Some of the monks looked a bit bleary-eyed and seemed to have a hard time chanting on key.

---

[24] Latin: "in room."

Following Matins, we filed into the refectory for breakfast, where we received another shock: Brother Tom was cooking again. "Where," said Brother Bob staring down at his bowl of glutenous, lukewarm porridge, "is Lucas?" Lucas was the chef the Abbot had hired away from a hotel in the Berkshires.

"Called to God," I replied, pushing the revolting bowl away and poured myself another cup of the liquid that passed for Brother Tom's coffee. I suspected that our espresso machine had been banished along with Lucas.

The Abbot was standing at the lectern reading to us, just as in the old days. There were bits of hay clinging to his cassock, a bit of "accessorizing"—as Elliott would have put it— for the benefit of Monsignor Maraviglia. The Abbot's text, insofar as I could tell, was from Saint Thad's lengthy discourse on the weaving of horsehair shirts. It is a highly technical passage, and I had a hard time following the Latin. Some of the other monks seemed either similarly baffled, or perhaps just too miserable to care, but Monsignor Maraviglia nodded approvingly along with the text. He even ate all his porridge, an impressive act of mortification in itself.

That afternoon the Abbot summoned me to his cell. I found him on his knees, not praying but stashing his Deepak Chopra books under the bed, which was strewn with hay.

"I'm not sure the hay is necessary," I said.

"You don't know Blutschpiller," he said. "Have you taken care of the car?" The Abbot had instructed me the night before to move his Lexus[25] from our garage to the Pilgrims Center parking lot.

"Yes."

[25] A luxury car not traditionally associated with monasteries.

He rummaged through his box. "Omigod," he said.

"What is it, Father?"

"Here—put these in the trunk of the car—and lock it." He handed me a large roll. I recognized it as the plans for the new golf course, to be built on neighboring farmland we had recently acquired.

"What's he doing now?" the Abbot asked.

"He's been in your suite—I mean, the Executive Retreat Center—all morning with Philomena."

"Have you been able to speak with her alone? Is she . . . cooperating?"

"I don't know," I said. "They seem to be getting along rather well."

Just then there was a knock on the door. It was Maraviglia. "Do I disturb?"

"Come in," said the Abbot. "Have a seat on the bed. If you don't mind the straw."

"Very admirable, Father." Maraviglia smiled. "But no thorns?"

"Difficult to find this time of year. Maybe in the fall."

Maraviglia was holding a sheaf of papers. "I found these in your suite. Excuse me, the guest suite. In the magazine rack next to the fireplace. Very interesting. What is 'Coverage'?"

Oh no, I thought. The Abbot, consumed with his various projects, had complained one day to Philomena that he was having a hard time keeping up with the daily breviary readings. She told him that in Hollywood executives had assistants who read everything for them and reduced books and movie scripts to two-page synopses called "coverage." The next day the Abbot ordered his new assistant Brother Mike to provide him with coverage of his daily Office.

Maraviglia read from a single sheet of paper, " 'Matins, Story of Prodigal Son. Two brothers—good guy, bad guy. Bad guy party animal, splits, blows dad's money, comes back with tail between legs. Dad says, Hey, no problem, let's party. Good son says, What's the deal here? I bust my chops, and he gets the party? Dad says, Chill—he's my son, he's back. There's a lot of love in this family."

The Abbot cleared his throat.

" 'Chill'?" said Maraviglia.

"Brother Mike has just joined us," said the Abbot. "He prepares these as part of his daily spiritual exercises. As you can see, he has not had extensive education. I told him to summarize the day's readings in his own language. 'Chill,' I think, here means to calm down."

Brilliant save, I thought.

MARAVIGLIA'S STAY—"OCCUPATION" might be the better word—entered its second month. He gave little indication of what horrors and heresies he was discovering in the course of his audit, cloistered in the Executive Retreat Center with Philomena. His only relaxation seemed to be watching Italian soccer in the Abbot's multimedia room. Amazingly, he had figured out how to program the satellite dish by himself; it had taken the Abbot three weeks to master.

We monks went about our monastic duties with renewed asceticism. At meals, the Abbot read to us from the writings of Saint Thad. He chose the most vivid passages from our patron's life of self-denial. One passage, which lasted over two meals, concerned which kind of salt was best to rub into one's freshly flagellated flesh. (Bavarian.) Another, containing a recipe for stew made from old sandals and horse bridles, did not improve the taste of Brother Tom's tuna casserole. We saw little of the Abbot between meals. He remained for the most part in his cell, seeking comfort in the works of Deepak Chopra.

I too kept out of Maraviglia's sights. I busied myself in my office monitoring the Cana Fund's performance on my computer screen, trying to concentrate on Latin American risk funds and Tokyo gold straddles. My mind was not entirely in the work. I missed Philomena. We had taken pains to maintain a chaste relationship—we had not repeated our moonlight embrace—but over the past year we had grown steadily closer. Our regular meetings to discuss Cana's affairs had been the high point of my day. But since the arrival of Maraviglia I had scarcely seen her.

One day, bored with tracking the price of platinum futures, I sought diversion surfing the Internet. I commanded the search engine to find sites pertaining to Saint Thaddeus, and soon found myself, amazingly enough, in a chat room devoted to *De Doloribus Extremis*. I watched the dialogue scrolling down the screen.

SGT. PAIN: Have u checked out chap iii where he's being tied up by the sultan's guards?

DOLORES DOLORIBUS: I LUVV that scene. HOT HOT HOT!!!

SGT. PAIN: You know u want it.

DOLORES DOLORIBUS: They forgot to gag him.

SGT. PAIN: Check out chap xxiii. Mother of all gags. Three pomegranates!!! Leave it to the Moors.

DOLORES DOLORIBUS: What's a pomegranate???

HORNY-THORNY: Chek out this dictionary def: "Fruit having a tough, reddish rind containing many seeds enclosed in a juicy, red pulp with acid flavor."

DOLORES DOLORIBUS: Acid! It hurtz so good!!!

SGT. PAIN: No wonder he went right on preaching after they let him go.

I immediately got myself out of that chat room. I had no idea that the founder of our order had such a following. Although their discussion shocked me, I had myself occasionally wondered at Saint Thad's propensity for getting himself into painful situations.

The Vatican's website offered no information on the Ufficio dell' Investigazione Interna but I did find something interesting in a multilingual chat room called alt.rel.rc .vatic.dish. It seemed to be full of gossipy Vatican insiders. As best as I could make out, they were speculating about who would get the contract for the upcoming renovation of Castel Gandolfo.[26] After they had spent ten minutes intensely debating the restoration of the *putti*[27] in the papal breakfast room, I waded in. Using my screen name, Hedgehog, I typed,

Know anything about Msgr. Maraviglia?

There was a pause.

---

[26] The Pope's summer residence, southeast of Rome.
[27] Cupid-like children depicted in Italian decorative arts, especially on ceilings.

PAGLIACCIO: Chi lo vuole sapere?[28]

HEDGEHOG: Speak English?

PAGLIACCIO: Of course. Why do you ask about Monsignor Maraviglia?

HEDGEHOG: Just curious. I've heard a lot about him.

PAGLIACCIO: The Monsignore is overseas on business.

HEDGEHOG: What kind of business?

PAGLIACCIO: Whatever Cardinal Blutschpiller requires, Maraviglia will do.

CALLISTUS: Whatever Cardinal Blutschpiller requires, the Pope will do.

URBANO: Who else would have dared to challenge the Holy Father's expense account!

HEDGEHOG: You're joking, right?

URBANO: No one jokes about Cardinal Blutschpiller. Why do you think there will be no Jacuzzi in the renovation of Castel Gandolfo? The Holy Father's physician even wrote a letter saying it was necessary for health reasons.

CALLISTUS: You remember what he said when he transferred Cardinal Montpellier from Paris to Kisangani?

HEDGEHOG: Actually not.

URBANO: "Condonat Deus, non Blutschpiller."[29]

HEDGEHOG: What's in Kisangani?

PAGLIACCIO: Lepers.

URBANO: And malaria.

HEDGEHOG: Why did Blutschpiller pick Maraviglia as his deputy?

---

[28] Italian: "Who wants to know?"
[29] Latin: "God forgives, not Blutschpiller."

BONIFACE: He wanted someone who knows the criminal mind. Before Maraviglia became a priest he was a man of the world.

HEDGEHOG: What did he do?

BONIFACE: Anything he wanted. He is from the Maraviglias of Milano, the textile family. His picture was always in the magazines with beautiful women—Monte Carlo, Lago di Como, Positano, Paris, New York, Palm Beach. Then the family fortune was finished. The business manager stole 26 billion lire,[30] and the father, Giancarlo, gambled away the remainder. So the playboy son became a priest with a great hatred for corruption in all forms. His severe manner attracted the attention of Blutschpiller. The Cardinal recognized in the young man the soul of a great inquisitor.

I heard a soft voice behind me say, "Research for the Hedge Fund, Brother?" I jumped in my seat. It was Philomena. She was peering over my shoulder at the screen. I quickly signed off.

"I didn't hear you come in."

"You were quite absorbed there. Who were you talking to?"

"I'm not sure. Some Vatican chat room. Whoever they are, they're all terrified of Blutschpiller. Even the Pope can't get a Jacuzzi without checking with him first. Apparently his henchman Maraviglia shares the Cardinal's views on mercy and forgiveness."

"Henchman? He's hardly that."

---

[30] About $15 million.

"Well, what would you call him? Lord High Executioner?"

"I call him Monsignor."

"Not on first-name basis yet? After all this time you've been spending together back there? This is turning out to be quite the audit."

"The Monsignor is a dedicated and holy man."

"Yeah, I noticed the halo. Blinding."

"I would have thought you'd respect someone with that kind of integrity."

"Integrity? Whoa. Let me get this straight. You're lecturing me about integrity? I seem to recall a sermon on a mount one evening from a certain MBA. The moral, I believe, was 'Hey, if it feels good and it makes money, go for it.' Tell me, did this newfound integrity reveal itself to you in a vision while you were hawking those firkin T-shirts at that Catholic Kmart of yours?"

She recoiled a bit. "Isn't pomposity a sin? What's gotten into you?"

"Forgive me if I'm a bit upset. I can't imagine why. Most people would be thrilled at the prospect of spending the rest of their lives ministering to lepers in the Congo."

"What are you talking about?"

"That's how Blutschpiller traditionally concludes his audits. And you, sitting there, helping him."

"I know the Cardinal is traditional—"

" *Traditional*'! In our Church, the rack is 'traditional.' Being broken on the wheel is 'traditional.' Having your fingernails ripped out one by—"

"Ty, relax. This isn't the fifteenth century. Look, Blutschpiller is Blutschpiller. But Maraviglia is different. You think it's easy for him to work for the Cardinal? He's actually a very sensitive man. He doesn't *enjoy* this."

"Oh," I said, "so he's been sharing his pain with you, has he? What else has he been sharing?"

She flushed. "So that's what this is all about. For a year now you've been playing the noble monk, invoking your sacred vow of chastity. And now you're jealous. How ... pathetic."

"Jealous? I'm just trying to figure out whose side you're on."

"Maybe I'm trying to sort it out myself."

"I'm sure the Monsignor can handle any spiritual questions much better than I could. I look like Richard Chamberlain only in the moonlight. He looks like him in daylight."

She looked hurt, but quickly recovered. "I don't have time to minister to a lovesick celibate monk." She stood up to go. "Why don't you go write a letter to Ann Landers."

I listened to the sound of her heels clicking down the marble corridor.

LATER THAT DAY, I recounted what I had learned about Maraviglia to the Abbot and the other monks in the library. We were all there for "study hour," a period the Abbot had added to our regular schedule in order to impress Maraviglia. He had ordered us to sit at the table with large, moldy tomes of Aquinas, Bede, and other Church fathers. For himself, he chose a folio-sized Latin Bible, big enough to hide whatever Chopran text he was studying.

The Abbot listened intently to my intelligence briefing. The old tension between us was gone now that we faced a common enemy.

"I'm not surprised he comes from a rich family," the Abbot said. "He certainly has excellent taste in wine."

"What do you mean?" I asked.

"He's gone through an entire case of Figeac."

"How do you know?"

The Abbot shrugged. "Someone has to check the cellar, turn the bottles...we can't let the whole R&D program come screeching to a halt."

"Extremely conscientious of you, Father Abbot."

"You can't just *abandon* good wine, you know. It has to be tended to, nurtured. It's a living thing, wine. It's like a child. The conditions must be exactly right, the humidity, the temperature..."

Brother Bob looked up from the atlas he had been studying. "It says here the average temperature in Kisangani is ninety-two degrees—that's during the cool season. The humidity seems to be fairly constant. Is one hundred percent humidity good for vintage Bordeaux?"

The Abbot's face darkened. "Where *is* Kisangani?"

Brother Bob was pointing it out to him when Maraviglia suddenly entered the room. He noticed the atlas opened to the map of equatorial Africa.

"So much work to be done in that part of the world," he said. "So much suffering, so many rigors. If Saint Thad were alive today, that is where he would be."

"Are you planning to visit the Dark Continent anytime soon?" the Abbot said hopefully from behind his Bible.

"If only that were possible," Maraviglia replied with that thin smile of his. "But who knows how long my work here will keep me."

"Only God," said the Abbot.

Maraviglia held up the book he was carrying, *Awaken the Giant Within,* by Anthony Robbins. "I found this in one of the pews in the chapel," he said. "Most interesting." He opened to two blank pages with the headings:

EMPOWERING BELIEFS   DISEMPOWERING BELIEFS

"Apparently the reader is supposed to fill in the pages himself."

Brother Gene, our leading Robbinite, spoke up. "It's a modern version of the illuminated book. The exercise has been very helpful for our monks."

The Monsignor nodded. "Tell me, who is this Anthony Robbins?"

"He's only the most important self-motivator of the twentieth century," said Brother Gene. This brought a snort from Brother Theo, our leading expert on Stephen Covey, author of *The Seven Habits of Highly Effective People.* Brother Theo's and Brother Gene's running argument over their respective subjects had divided the monks into camps. At one point, the Coveyans stopped speaking to the Robbinites, even refusing to exchange the ceremonial kiss of peace during the Mass.

"Robbins?" Brother Theo harrumphed. "Anthony Robbins, who goes around walking on hot coals like some Indian fakir? Monsignor, he actually does this at his seminars to show people that they can do anything if they put their minds to it. I don't know if he did this for the President at Camp David. But I certainly hope our Commander in Chief was not induced to follow his other advice about what to do when you're depressed. He advises his followers to jump up and down and shout, "Hallelujah! My feet don't stink today!"

Brother Gene rose to the defense of his guru. "Anthony Robbins has sold twenty-four million videocassettes. His technique may be emotionally based, but for many this works much better than the pseudo-cerebralism of Stephen R. Covey, with his Time-Management Matrix and Circles of Proactive Focus."

As the theological dispute raged, a look of puzzlement came over Monsignor Maraviglia. He strolled over to the shelves, which now housed what was probably the finest private collection of first editions of such classics as Benjamin Franklin's *Poor Richard's Almanac* and Dale Carnegie's *How to Win Friends and Influence People*. In amassing the collection, the Abbot had cleaned out the Self-Help section of several large bookstores. The modern canon included hundreds upon hundreds of books, from *Trump: The Art of the Deal* to *Wealth Without Risk* to *Think and Grow Rich*.

Maraviglia contemplated the Chopran collection, by far the largest. He pulled a thin, well-thumbed book from the shelf. I recognized it instantly: *Creating Affluence*, the Abbot's urtext.

"His masterpiece," the Abbot said. "Not as systematic, perhaps, as *The Seven Spiritual Laws of Success*, but infinitely more accessible." The Robbinites sitting at the table rolled their eyes.

Maraviglia opened the book and read. " 'S stands for spending . . . money is like blood; it must flow.' " He shook his head. "I am not sure I understand."

"Welcome to the club," said Brother Gene. "If you want clear thinking on spending, turn to Robbins' five-step program—"

"Oh, please," the Abbot snorted. "Don't listen to him, Monsignor. If you want empty cheerleading, by all means, read Robbins. If you want idiotic diagrams, read Covey. If you want results, read Chopra."

Maraviglia gave the Abbot a hard look. "What 'results' can you mean?"

"*Si monumentum requiris circumspice,*"[31] the Abbot replied. "Without Deepak Chopra, there would be no Mount Cana, no pilgrims, no winery, to say nothing of the Executive Retreat Center that you seem to find so...accommodating."

Maraviglia's eyes turned steely. " 'Spending must flow like blood'? Where, exactly in Holy Scripture, did Our Lord encourage us to spend money extravagantly? I am sure Cardinal Blutschpiller would be interested to hear you reconcile Chopra with the Church."

I feared that the Abbot was not up to scriptural debate with one of the Pope's top lieutenants. As far as I knew, it had been months since he had bothered to read more than Brother Mike's "coverage" of biblical readings. But that gave him ammunition.

"Surely the Monsignor has not forgotten the very passage we discussed in my cell recently. The story of the Prodigal Son, who was rewarded by his father for his generous spending." He turned to Brother Bob with a superior air and said, "Would you be kind enough to give the Monsignor the exact citation?"

---

[31] The epitaph of Christopher Wren, architect of Saint Paul's cathedral in London: "If you seek his monument, look about you."

"Luke 15:11–32," said Brother Bob. The monks oohed respectfully.

"Luke 12:15," Maraviglia immediately countered. In the deadly silence we could hear Brother Bob flipping backward through the pages of the New Testament. He read the verse aloud: " 'Take heed, and beware of covetousness: for a man's life consisteth not in the abundance of the things which he possesseth.' "

The Abbot's brow furrowed. He was digging deep into his pre-Deepakian neural bank.

"Deuteronomy...8..." *Come on, come on,* I thought. He smiled. "Yes. Deuteronomy 8:10."

Brother Bob flipped furiously. He read: " 'When thou hast eaten and art full, then thou shalt bless the Lord thy God for the good land which He hath given thee.' "

The monks murmured excitedly.

"Timothy 6:6–10," said Maraviglia. "Check and—if I am not mistaken, Father Abbot—mate."

Brother Bob read the citation somberly. " 'They that will be rich fall into temptation and hurtful lusts, which drown men in destruction and perdition.' "

Suddenly the room felt oppressively warm, not unlike Kisangani. We looked imploringly at the Abbot. Sweat was trickling down his temple.

Maraviglia turned. He strolled to the bookcase and shoved *Creating Affluence* in among the others. He began to walk out of the room. Just as he was about to disappear through the door the Abbot's voice stopped him cold. "Ecclesiastes 6:1–2." The Abbot smiled at the Monsignor. The Monsignor did not smile back.

It seemed an eternity before Brother Bob read the passage: " 'There is an evil which I have seen under the sun, and it is common: a man to whom God hath given wealth, but the man cannot spend it because a' "—Brother Bob looked up at Maraviglia as he said the next word—" '*stranger* has moved into his house to enjoy it. . . .' "

The Abbot finished the citation. "This is *vanity*, and it is an evil disease."

Maraviglia looked at us. For a moment, I thought he might excommunicate us on the spot. But then we saw the thin smile.

"Bravo, Father Abbot," he said. "I will toast you tonight." He paused. "With a Pétrus '61."

"Not the Pé—" the Abbot started to say, but Maraviglia was already out the door.

As soon as he was out of earshot, we gave the Abbot a round of applause.

I still had my doubts about Chopra, but I had to hand it to the Abbot. There was an unmistakable parallel between Deepak and Ecclesiastes. At that moment in the library I grasped the Fifth Law of Spiritual and Financial Growth:

V.

MONEY WON'T MAKE YOU HAPPY UNLESS YOU SPEND IT.

Market Meditation
the Fifth

Did not *buying something nice ever make me happy?*
Did I ever see a gorgeous, expensive car in a
showroom and say to myself, What a waste of
money buying that would be!?
Am I really saying, I'm not good enough for that car?
Does God think that car is too good for me?
Does God drive around in a '78 Corolla?
How long has it been since I went out and really splurged
on something nice?
What's stopping me from doing it right now?
"INSUFFICIENT FUNDS"?
What about the saying "You have to spend *money*
in order to make *money"?*

Your questions are simply dazzling. You're making amazing progress. Now, gather up all your recent credit-card receipts. (Do *not* fold them into paper airplanes!) Go through each purchase carefully, and ask yourself, Did buying this leave me with a happy feeling? Or did it leave me with a *really* happy feeling? Then put it into one of two piles: HAPPY and REALLY HAPPY. Take out a pencil, calculator, and piece of paper. (IMPORTANT! Do *not* use the paper airplane for this purpose!) Okay. Add up the total purchase price for each pile. Ready? Take your time.... Your two piles might look something like this:

HAPPY	*REALLY HAPPY*
$32 electric nasal hair remover	*$412 mink-lined toilet-seat cover*
$26 carton of cigarettes	*$1,330 diamond zodiac-sign pendant*
$72 pistol (Czech-made, .22 caliber)	*$2,750,000 cabin cruiser (turbocharged)*
$130 Total	*$2,751,742 Total*

Okay, *now* divide the total of each pile by the number of receipts in that pile to find the Average Price Per Item.™ Take time to check your math carefully. For the examples above, the APPI™ for the HAPPY pile would be $43.33. The APPI™ for the REALLY HAPPY pile would be $917,247.33. Your actual numbers may be different—that's okay. But by now you have noticed a *crucial difference between the two piles:* REALLY HAPPY costs a whole lot more than HAPPY. If this isn't the case, go back and check your math, or call your credit-card company and have your card canceled immediately!

Does it all "seem to fit"? You bet it does. This is known as the First Corollary to the Fifth Law™: the more money you spend, the happier you'll be.

Prayer of the Cheerful Spender

*Heavenly Father, Processor of all transactions, grant
that all my credit-card purchases be swiftly
approved, no matter how humble my bank balance.
Let me neither hoard my funds here on earth,
nor hide my wallet under a bushel. And keep strangers from
my door, lest they partake of riches that would be better
spent on myself. Let me be as the Prodigal Son,
disbursing his father's money with an open heart,
living life to the fullest, eschewing thrift and employment,
and when day is done and all the money is spent
and clamorous creditors pursue me through the streets,
welcome me back into Thy House with open arms.*

CHAPTER THE SIXTH

An Unlucky Pilgrim...
The Monsignor Unwinds...
A Ghost named Sebastian...
Rome Rumbles...
A Terrible Surprise

HE NEXT MONTH BROUGHT one tribulation after another. *Wine Spectator,* one of the leading wine magazines in the country, gave Abbot's Own a rating of 72 out of a possible 100. The reviewer noted its "unusually high price for an upstate New York cabernet," and described its taste as a mixture of "blackberry, avocado, and overripe bananas, not a heavenly combination." Frank Prial of *The New York Times,* also marveling at its "mountainous price," said it was "strangely reminiscent of some of the heartier table wines from Chile's Maipo Valley." (Prial certainly knew his Chilean wines.) Orders for Abbot's Own fell dramatically, and kept slipping even after we reduced the price.

Then there was the accident. Brother Jerome was conducting a wine tasting for a group of pilgrims—Knights of Columbus from Buffalo, New York—and, somewhere between the fifth and sixth glasses, announced that "wine takes us closer to God!" One of the inebriated Knights apparently took the remark literally. He wandered off and began climbing the still-unfinished path up the side of Mount Cana. He got as far as the Shrine of Saint Thad, where he somehow pitched forward over the railing into the pit of brambles, where he underwent mortification for a half hour before his cries were heard. The $20 million lawsuit noted the plaintiff's seventy-eight stitches, as well as the "severe emotional distress resulting from being subjected to medieval torture." Several large pilgrim tour groups canceled after the headline in the Buffalo paper: KNIGHT'S NIGHTMARE AT CANA WINERY.

We had been anticipating revenue from the Cana Cask-Ade water ride, which was supposed to open in time for the summer season, but the project was behind schedule and over budget. Elliott was having problems feeding the custom-made Cana Red dye into the giant firkin near the top. The dye kept leaking into the system that made snow for the peak. As a result, Mount Cana looked less like a majestic alp than a half-melted cherry snow cone. "For alps," Elliott explained, "you basically want white."

The bills from our lawyers, construction companies, and Chilean wine suppliers were piling up on my desk. One afternoon I went to discuss our financial problems with Monsignor Maraviglia, who had taken control of our accounts.

When I entered the executive suite, I was surprised to find the Monsignor watching television, with an opened bottle of fine Château Duhart-Milon Rothschild on the coffee table. He was watching a soccer game on the large screen. I cleared my throat to announce my presence. He glanced at me and waved me to sit down.

"I do not usually relax so early in the day," he said without taking his eyes off the screen, "but today is special. My team, AC Milan, is playing Stuttgart."

I tried to fathom the enormity of Milan playing Stuttgart. "Stuttgart?" I said.

"The Cardinal's team," he whispered. *"And we are one goal ahead."* I had never seen him look so pleased. He provided me with a running commentary on the individual magnificence of each Milanese player. When Stuttgart's star forward, Willi Becker, had to be carried off the field after a vicious slide tackle, Maraviglia could barely contain his glee.

"Blutschpiller must be devastated," he said excitedly. "Becker is his favorite. We shall drink to this!"

Before I could protest, he had gotten another glass and filled it. He handed it to me and clinked his against it. "To victory over Germany!"

I didn't want to drink, but I thought it politic to join in the Monsignor's celebration. I took a sip. It was delicious. Maraviglia drained his glass and poured himself another, emptying the bottle. It was not yet three in the afternoon. No wonder he was so relaxed.

"Do you and the Cardinal watch games together in the Vatican?" I asked.

"Bravo, Mario!" he yelled at the screen. "Yes, we watch, sometimes."

"That must be nice."

"Not if his team is losing. When he is unhappy, it is best to be somewhere else. Today it is good to have the Atlantic Ocean between him and me." He sipped his wine. "In truth," he said with a hint of levity, "there are many days when it is good to have an ocean between us."

I didn't care about soccer, but this was getting interesting. I took another sip to keep him company. "I imagine working for the Cardinal isn't easy."

"Easy? Hah!" Noticing the bottle was drained, he got up and disappeared down the steps into the Abbot's wine cellar. He emerged a moment later with another bottle of $150 Lafite Rothschild. Somewhere, the Abbot was weeping.

"You know, Brother Ty, I have come to appreciate the seclusion of your monastic way. It is very tranquil here. To be truthful, I am not in a great hurry to return to the pressures of the Vatican. I am enjoying my time with you."

As he decanted the new bottle on the sideboard I caught sight of a familiar videocassette box next to the VCR.

"Have you been watching *The Thorn Birds*?" I asked.

"We are up to the part where the priest gets the old lady's money," he said, returning to the couch with the decanter. "Tell me something. Do you think I resemble this actor Richard Chamberlain?"

"I really couldn't say. I've been told I look like him myself."

Maraviglia studied me for a moment. "No," he said, "I don't see it."

"Well," I said, stiffening, "I didn't come here to talk about Richard Chamberlain. Our checking account is depleted. If

we're to pay our bills, we'll need to tap the reserve funds.
We'll need about—"

"Fermatelo! Fermatelo! No! No! Nooo!"[32]

I looked at the screen. Stuttgart had scored. Maraviglia
collapsed back onto the leather sofa. The game was now
tied, with only minutes left to play. In the last seconds,
Stuttgart scored the winning goal on a corner kick. Maraviglia slammed his wineglass on the table with such force
that the bottom snapped off.

"Porca miseria! Li mortacci tua!"[33]

I knew that Europeans took their soccer seriously, but the
Monsignor's shock seemed a bit out of proportion. I began
to suspect that this had less to do with soccer than with his
feelings toward Blutschpiller.

"Perhaps," I said, getting up, "this isn't the right time to
discuss finances."

Maraviglia seemed embarrassed. In a businesslike way, he
said, "No, now is fine. You say you need more money?"

"Yes. To pay bills."

"I cannot approve any disbursement from the reserve
fund. If you need money, you will have to raise it some other
way." He stood up to indicate that the conversation was over.
"I hear you are very good at raising money, Brother Ty."

I STORMED OFF to the Pilgrim's Center in search of Philomena. Unsteady from the wine, I bumped into a child who
was standing with his family at the cash register, about to

---

[32] Italian: "Stop him! Stop him! No! No! Nooo!"
[33] Italian, literally: "Miserable pig! May all your relatives die!"

buy a battery-operated action toy, an Expiator 2. It clattered to the floor and switched itself on. The plastic Saint Thad began advancing on its knees, its right arm beating its breast as the recorded voice repeated, *"Mea culpa! Mea culpa! Mea maxima culpa!"*[34]

"MEA culpa!" I said to the boy as I reached down to pick up his toy. Somehow I lost my balance and pitched forward, crushing Saint Thad's head with my kneecap. To my considerable embarrassment, I had to be helped to my feet by the boy's father as he consoled his hysterical son. The headless torso of Saint Thad kept repeating "meameameamea..."

"He cut Saint Thad's head off!" screamed the child.

"There, there," said the father, "we'll get you a new one."

"On the house," I groaned, rubbing my knee. I said to the child, "You know, that's how the real Saint Thad met his end."

"Someone stepped on him?" the boy asked.

I told Brother Algernon behind the cash register to give him a free Expiator 2. Then I limped upstairs to Philomena's suite.

"What happened to you?" she said.

"One of your action dolls attacked me. Can I sit down?"

She came around her desk and helped me to a seat. She must have caught a whiff of my breath.

"*Ty.* Drinking again? In the *afternoon?*"

"I was with Monsignor."

"Are you okay?" she said with concern. "Is something wrong?"

---

[34] Line from the Latin Mass meaning, "Through my fault, through my fault, through my most grievous fault."

"Very wrong," I said.

"What?"

"Stuttgart won."

She looked at me. "What are you talking about?"

"We were watching TV together. Just the two of us—three of us, if you count Baron Rothschild. Very cozy, though we were only watching soccer. We didn't get a chance to watch *The Thorn Birds*. But I guess he saves that for someone else," I said. "Someone who tells him how much he looks like Richard Chamberlain."

"Honestly, Ty."

"He seems quite pleased by the comparison."

"Well, he *does* look like him. I can't help that."

"I see. You were just being honest with him. Helping him with the audit. Part of your fiducenary—fidu … responsibility. *Oo, Monsignore mio! Have I told you in the last ten minutes how much you look like Richard Chamberlain?*"

"Okay, so we watched *The Thorn Birds* one night. Big deal. We were exhausted. We'd spent ten hours looking at spreadsheets. Blutschpiller called three times to scream at him. I could hear him from across the room. Can you imagine the pressure he's under? He's got the original boss from hell."

"And you're doing everything you can to help them. You're on Team Blutschpiller. Building the case that will send us to the Congo. Don't you feel *any* guilt? *You're* the one who dreamed up most of these scams. The Miracle of Cana! Firkin T-shirts! Action-toy martyrs!" My knee throbbed.

"Maybe I was wrong. Some of the changes around here have not exactly been to the greater glory of God. All this chasing after the almighty buck ... I've been giving it a lot of thought lately. Working with Ray has made me—"

"Ray? Who is Ray?"

Philomena blushed. "I meant, the Monsignor."

"Oh, *that* Ray. Raffaello Chamberlain. Of course."

"Ty, would you just get *over* it?"

"Sorry. I just don't have your facility for easy transitions. But then I took a vow of chastity."

"I have work to do," she said. "I don't have to listen to a drunk monk."

I lifted myself painfully off the chair and hobbled to the door. I struggled to come up with a valedictory riposte, something rapierlike, worthy of Oscar Wilde. I turned with a flourish on reaching the door.

"Well, firk *you*."

A FEW DAYS later the Abbot summoned me, Philomena, and Brent, our director, to a meeting. It was a bit cramped in his cell with the four of us. Brent was fascinated by the straw. "Is this a health thing?" he asked.

"No," said the Abbot, "it's a poverty thing."

"I thought you were over that."

"That's what we're here to discuss. Orders are off, expenses are up. We need to generate some income stream. We need some new ideas. We need to put the miracle back into Cana."

Philomena was the first to speak. "Monsignor feels we should be concentrating on making better wine."

The Abbot and I rolled our eyes. The Abbot said, "Why? Has he gone through all our Bordeaux already?"

"Quod seris metes," she said.

"I loved that movie," said Brent. "There's never been a Nero like Ustinov."

"That's *Quo Vadis,*" Philomena said.

"Philomena is very up on her Latin these days," I said. "She's been getting private lessons."

"It means, 'Reap as you sow,' " she continued, ignoring me. "What Monsignor means is that if we make good wine, we won't have to worry about marketing."

A loud hush fell over the room.

"It's something to think about," she said.

"Okay," said the Abbot. "Now that we've thought about it, let's move on to the wolf howling at the door. Brent?"

"We could do another straight commercial. Miracle two—new-improved, bigger-better. But I'm sensing here that we've got a quality-control problem. We've got to ask ourselves—who's going to buy into it? People have tried this wine. They know what it tastes like. Face it, we're never going to get the serious wine-heads. They read the reviews, they know it sucks. No offense."

"It's perfectly drinkable Chilean table wine," said the Abbot.

"Right, and you've got to find people who are happy with that. We're not talking about supersophisticated people, okay? And that's fine. The less they know, the better. If they can't even read the label, hey, great—we're talking huge market."

"Stupid people, in other words," said the Abbot.

"There's your new slogan," said Philomena, " 'Cana, the wine to serve when your guests are too dumb to know the difference.' "

"Exactly," Brent said. "And for that, you don't want a straight commercial, you want an infomercial. Forget the high-priced spots on *Sound of Music*. For a fraction of that you can buy thirty straight minutes on late-night cable."

"Is that the cost-effective way to reach stupid people?" I asked.

"Exactly," said Brent. "I know it's hard to believe they actually work. I was a doubter myself until I did the Ricardo Montalban infomercial on Fatima." He turned to the Abbot, "Did you catch it?"

"I'm afraid not," said the Abbot. I wasn't sure he would have admitted it if he had.

"At first I thought, Wow, we have nothing—I mean, *nada*—to work with. We've got a shrine somewhere in Portugal, where a bunch of kids say they saw the Virgin Mary a long time ago. We got a few stories of cures and twirling lights in the sky, basically because these peasants stared too long at the sun. And for a host they give me an actor who's been hawking Corinthian leather upholstery for a living. I'm thinking, this is *never* going to work. But it did."

"What are you proposing for Cana?" Philomena asked.

"I was thinking Sally Field."

"The Flying *Nun*? You can't be serious."

"Why not? Imagine her taking a big gulp of wine and saying, 'You'll like it! You'll *really* like it!' "

"But even assuming you do get Sally Field, they won't like it," Philomena said. "Marketing isn't everything. It's the wine they have to like."

The Abbot reached out and touched Philomena's arm. He looked at her with concern. "Are you all right?"

✠

WE NEVER DID get Sally Field, of course, but we did get Hugh O'Toole. His career had peaked three decades earlier when he starred in *Holy Ghost!*, the television series about the parish priest whose confessional is haunted by a mischievous ghost named Sebastian who gets him out of—but mostly into—trouble by staging miracles. (Fred MacMurray played the continually irritated bishop.)

Filming took a week. For the opening shot, Brent's crew built a replica of the confessional in *Holy Ghost!* O'Toole had a bit of a hard time squeezing into it, owing to the extra weight he had put on. But he slipped right back into his old character as he sat there listening to a tape-recorded voice coming through the screen.

"Bless me, Father, for I have found the best wine ever made!" said the familiar, squeaky voice of Sebastian the Ghost. "Rich, full-bodied, aromatic yet tasty, fruity yet sophisticated, prepared by holy hands and available at a heavenly price!"

"Sebastian!" O'Toole hissed, "How many times have I told you to stay out of the confessional?"

"But, Father, you have to try this wine!"

"Not in the confessional!" At this, two technicians with fishing poles lowered a bottle of Cana and a wineglass in front of the priest. On seeing the levitating objects, O'Toole did his trademark double take and plaintive cry: "Please, Sebastian—not *another* miracle!"

O'Toole reached for the bottle, which then flitted out of his grasp. Following it out of the confessional, he was led to

Cana's front door. The bottle knocked on the door, which was opened by a beaming Abbot. He cheerfully took O'Toole on a tour of the winery—leaving out the Executive Retreat Center. O'Toole pretended to marvel as the Abbot answered such hard-hitting questions as "How do you get the wine to taste so divine?"

"Three things. Hard work, good grapes, and a drop of something special we've formulated here at Cana." He pointed to the machine that dispensed a drop of actual Cana wine into each bottle on the conveyor.

"What is it?" O'Toole asked.

"Well," the Abbot said with a cherubic wink, "let's just say it's a secret ingredient we call . . . *love.*"

I wondered if it was a good idea to emphasize this particular aspect of our operation. Aside from being potentially embarrassing—I imagined the headline, MONKS' SECRET INGREDIENT: BAD WINE—it might arouse the interest of our old friends at the Bureau of Alcohol, Tobacco and Firearms. Talk of "secret ingredients" might be construed as a health claim, a serious violation of federal law. I brought this problem to the attention of the Abbot and Brent.

"Don't you worry about the BATF," the Abbot said. "They wouldn't dare come after a community of poor monks on a ridiculous technicality. I put the fear of God into that agent."

"He didn't look that scared to me," I said.

The Abbot gave a stern look. "Brother, don't you have a hedge fund to attend to? Your last quarter's performance was somewhat disappointing."

This was, clearly, my cue to withdraw. I spent the next two weeks obediently staring at the computer screen, fretting as the dollar dropped against the deutsche mark. In the calefactory after dinner, I heard snatches of gossip about the filming: the building of a new grotto at the foot of Mount Cana, busloads of extras brought in from New York, heated arguments between Philomena and Brent. "Be thankful you aren't involved in this one," said Brother Bob one evening. "They are having what are called 'serious creative differences.' "

WE HAD TO stay up until 1:00 A.M. to see the infomercial debut. I was sleepy, and almost drifted off as I watched the Abbot lead Hugh O'Toole on his tour, but when they walked past a rather large mound of crutches, I sat bolt upright.

"What are those?" I whispered to Brent, sitting next to me.

"Crutches," he said.

"I know they're crutches. What are they doing there?"

"It's just a quick visual way of saying 'Shrine.' You want them thinking Lourdes, Fatima."

"Why?"

"Just watch. This next scene is going to make you weep."

The Abbot and O'Toole paused at the foot of Mount Cana next to the grotto Brent's prop crew had devised. In the middle of the pool was a large bottle of Cana spouting red wine. A group of pilgrims stood by, filling their wineglasses from the spout, murmuring among themselves.

"Great bouquet!"

"I feel ten years younger!"

"Velvety finish!"

"I've lost fifteen pounds!"

"I don't get it—how can they sell premium wine like this for under ten dollars?"

"I can walk again!"

The Abbot and O'Toole stopped to have a chat with a young woman named Brenda, who had just tossed her crutches into the pile. She perkily explained that she had been contemplating suicide until hearing about Cana wine from a friend whose eyesight had been restored after he drank a case of it.

"That's wonderful!" O'Toole said to the girl, as he accepted a salmon puff pastry from a monk circulating with a tray of hors d'oeuvres. Turning to the Abbot, O'Toole asked earnestly, "Father Abbot, tell us, how could wine heal all these people?"

"Now, Hugh," said the Abbot, "we here at Cana don't think of ourselves as being in the healing business. All we try to do is make a great wine at a great price. Miracles like the one that happened to Brenda here and these other folks could only come from God."

At this, a squeaky voice piped up: "Or me!"

"Quiet, Sebastian!" O'Toole ordered.

The Abbot led O'Toole (and Sebastian) up Mount Cana, warning him as they passed the Shrine of Saint Thad, "Careful of those brambles, Hugh, unless you're in the mood for some serious mortification."

"Not today, thanks."

"Ouch!" said Sebastian. "Now I'll have to get a new sheet!"

At the top, they got into one of the Cana Cask-Ade boats. The Abbot uncorked a bottle of Abbot's Own. There was a fuss as Sebastian insisted on sitting in the front. His presence there was indicated by a hovering glass of wine.

"So, Father Abbot," said O'Toole, as they looked off into the sunset over the vineyards, "tell us—can you and the monks make enough of this marvelous wine to share with all the people who want to buy it?"

"We're sure trying, Hugh. But I can't say how long our supplies will last."

"So people who want to order this great wine should do it right away, without wasting a *minute*?"

"Exactly, Hugh. They should call the number at the bottom of the screen. For a limited time, we'll even throw in a replica of the famous firkin jugs used by Our Lord at the wedding feast at Cana. Our monks are standing by. They take all major credit cards. Even minor ones."

"And what if they want to come to Cana? Is this a place the entire family could have fun visiting?"

Sebastian said, "What's this lever here do?"

"Don't touch anything!" said O'Toole, but the lever next to the front seat swung backward.

"Hang on," said the Abbot.

"Oh, no!" said O'Toole as the boat began to slide forward toward the edge of the flume. *"Sebastiiiiiiiiaaaaaaaan!"*

The cask hurtled down the flume, and landed at the bottom in a splash of wine-colored water.

The crowd by the grotto cheered, threw off their remaining crutches, and began running up the mountain.

"Now *this* is what I call a miracle!" said Sebastian, as his hovering wineglass tipped and emptied.

The infomercial ended. We could hear a carillon of phones ringing in the Fulfillment Center next door. "Listen to that," said Brent, breaking into song. "The hills are a-live ... with the sound of mo-ney!"

WITHIN A MONTH we had taken orders for 150,000 cases of Cana, and were averaging 2,300 pilgrims a day. After paying off the bills, we still had $10 million in the bank. A tanker carrying Chilean cabernet was steaming to New York. The Abbot basked in Cana's renewed fame, giving tours to reporters and VIPs (Very Important Pilgrims), and began conferring with Elliott about his latest scheme, which he called the Baths of Cana. I didn't want to hear about it, but Elliott told me that it involved "a total immersion experience in piping hot wine." He and the Abbot tried to get Philomena to work up a business plan for their new spa and line of CanaCare™ health and beauty products, but she said she was too busy tending to the flood of pilgrims. As for Monsignor Maraviglia, he was pointedly silent about recent developments. He made no mention of the infomercial, the growing mound of crutches by the grotto, or when he would finish his seemingly interminable audit.

One morning Brother Mike, the Abbot's assistant, came to see me with a letter from the Bureau of Alcohol, Tobacco and Firearms. It was addressed to the Abbot.

"He told me to throw this away," said Brother Mike. "But I thought you might want to check it out first."

I read:

With reference to recent televised promotion for Cana wine product, this will constitute formal notification that said promotion is in violation of the Code of Federal Regulations, volume 27, section

4.39, subsection h, forbidding any statement that
"the use of wine has curative or therapeutic effects
if such statement is untrue in any particular or
tends to create a misleading impression." Under
category of claim of therapeutic benefit is specifically included:

- restored ambulation;
- weight loss;
- new hair growth;
- relief from anxiety;
- dermatological benefits;
- increased sexual vigor;
- restored vision.

You are hereby summoned to appear at the office listed above to answer these charges. It is rec-
ommended that you be accompanied by legal
counsel. You may dispute the charges and at that
time present such evidence as you deem support-
ive of your position.

Be further advised that this office has previously
been in receipt of complaints by consumers alleg-
ing nonfulfillment of telephone and/or mail orders
of your product.

In addition, be advised that complaints have
been raised about the accuracy of your product's
label. BATF regulations specify that the words
"produced by" can only be used for products that
meet strict requirements.

You may address these additional areas of concern at the scheduled hearing referenced above.

Penalties for conviction of above infractions include substantial fines, confiscation of property,
and imprisonment.

I looked up at Brother Mike. "The Abbot told you to
throw this away?"

Brother Mike shrugged. "Yeah. He's been kinda casual
about getting back to people. *60 Minutes*[35] has called half a
dozen times now. Some lady saying she's Mike Wallace's
producer."

"*60 Minutes?*" I said. "Oh, great. Just what we need. Mike
Wallace, investigating the 'secret ingredient of Cana'—
fraud."

"Yeah," said Brother Mike. "Maybe best not to return
those calls. But I don't know why he's ignoring BATF. When
I asked him, he said, 'Oh, they're just trying to scare us
again.' Apparently, the bureau was here a year ago or something?"

"Yes. We had a conversation about unfulfilled orders.
They certainly scared me, but you know the Abbot. He an-
swers to a higher authority."

"Yeah, render unto Caesar. I did a coverage on that. Did
you catch the hearing date?"

To my dismay, the date was a week past. Brother Mike
pointed out that the letter had been mailed the day after the

---

[35] Highly popular television news magazine known for its investigations and exposés. Its
star reporter, Mike Wallace, is known for his "ambush interviews."

infomercial ran. Clearly, the Abbot had more urgent things on his plate than to answer a summons from a federal law enforcement agency.

I immediately called BATF and reached the agent who had been to Cana. He listened in silence to my profuse apology and request for a new hearing date. On the matter of the health claims, I tried arguing that the Abbot had included a disclaimer in the infomercial.

"You can try telling that to the hearing officer," he said, unmoved. "Assuming I can get you a new hearing date. I'll do what I can. But I gotta tell you, Cana isn't in great standing around here. We're getting complaints again about you not filling orders."

"Don't worry," I said. "We'll be shipping those orders soon. The wine's on the way here."

"On the way?" he said. "On the way from where?"

"Uh, from the vats. To the bottles. We've been having a few production problems."

"When do you expect to have those problems fixed?"

"Any day now," I said, guessing wildly. "A week, tops."

"Are you guaranteeing that?"

"Do I have to?"

"It would help, getting you a new hearing date."

"Then I guarantee it."

"Okay. One week. Friday the seventeenth. Noon? You'll have product coming off the line?"

"Absolutely."

"Good, then you won't mind if we have an agent there to verify that."

There was no time to lose. I called the winery in Chile. They checked with their shipper and gave me good news the freighter was due into New York the next day. The wine would be off-loaded over the weekend and clear customs Monday. As soon as they received the balance of the payment—we still owed $2 million—they would release the wine. I got Maraviglia to fax our bank in New York, authorizing the wire transfer to Chile Monday morning. I also called the trucking company and said we needed the wine Monday night. The truckers of course demanded a "cash bonus" since it would mean working an actual eight-hour day.

I was still at my computer an hour later, working on the Cana hedge fund when I got an E-mail message. It was from Pagliaccio, one of the regulars in the Vatican chat room. We had become E-buddies. Today he had some truly hot news:

> *Caro Hedgehog,*
>   *Our Scarlet Friend is going to America next week.*
> *His personal secretary, Father Hans, made the arrange-*
> *ments Wednesday after the weekly staff meeting. At*
> *the meeting they showed him a video of an American*
> *monastery that makes wine. It's the same one that made*
> *His Holiness ill. Now the monks say their wine cures*
> *every kind of ailment. Imagine! Perhaps they will bring*
> *it with them to Kisangani. Maybe it will also cure their*
> *malaria!*

So Blutschpiller was on the way. Maraviglia's audit was finally over. The videotape must have been the last bit of damning evidence in his report, and now the Great Excommunicator himself was coming to officiate at our day of judgment. Maraviglia was just doing his job, but he might at least have warned us. For that matter, why hadn't Philomena told us that a date had been set for our executions? I went off to the executive conference center.

They were both there, eating lunch at the table, enjoying a nice bottle of Barolo.

"How cozy," I said. "Barolo. The perfect complement to a completed audit."

Philomena looked up from her lasagna. "If only it were over. Between the pilgrims and the audit, I'm not getting much sleep these days."

Tempted as I was, I decided not to pursue a discussion of her nocturnal activities. "Not finished *yet?* Well, I suppose there are always last-minute details, like deciding what kind of firewood to use."

They both stared at me. Maraviglia said, "I do not comprehend."

"For the burning of the heretics at the stake. Tell me, Monsignor, what kind *does* Cardinal Blustschpiller prefer? We'd better lay in a good supply for his arrival next week."

They both looked startled. Obviously, I wasn't supposed to know. "I have to say, when I heard he was coming, I felt a little...hurt. I said to myself, Always the last to know. So why didn't you tell us? I thought we had a relationship. After all the"—I shot Philomena a glance—"good times we've shared, after all the great wine, you might have told us Blutschpiller's on his way here."

"Who told you that?" said Maraviglia.

"Oh, I have my sources. I hear it was quite a lively staff meeting on Wednesday. Apparently the Cardinal was so thrilled by our infomercial that he had Father Hans book him on a flight next week. He must want some of our wine for his prostate. Why didn't he just call? Our operators are standing by."

Maraviglia dabbed his mouth with the napkin and stood up. He walked to the window and gazed out on Mount Cana. In the distance, we could see pilgrims at Saint Thad's shrine, tossing coins into the brambles. Above, a caskload of junior pilgrims hurtled down the flume, their shrieks of pleasure faintly audible through the glass.

I looked over at Philomena. She was staring intently at Maraviglia. "Is this *true*, Ray?"

Finally he turned, and said, "I was not at liberty to say anything."

"So the audit is over," she said, struggling to control herself. I could see it dawning on her that her Monsignor would soon be leaving. This episode of *The Thorn Birds* was coming to a close. Now *she* knew what it felt like to be dumped. Part of me felt sorry for her. Another part of me was saying: *Good*.

"Well," she said, "I'm glad someone told me."

For the first time, Maraviglia seemed to be the most uncomfortable one in the room. "Philo*mee*na," he said in the pleading tone of an unfaithful lover who had just been caught, "I *wanted* to tell you."

He caught the smirk on my face. "I wanted to tell all of you. But the Cardinal insisted on absolute secrecy."

"What happens now?" Philomena asked. "When does he arrive?"

"Ask Brother Ty. He seems to know everything. Tell us, what flight does he arrive on?"

"I'm sorry"—I smiled—"but I'm not at liberty to say."

"Oh, honestly," she said, "would one of you men of God *please* tell me what's going on." Neither Maraviglia nor I budged. "I get it—no girls allowed in the treehouse. Just like the Church."

"Cardinal's orders," said Maraviglia. He turned to me. "I will consult with Rome about this development. I will make an announcement at dinner tonight. In the meantime, you will please respect the authority of the Holy See. Discuss this with no one. Will you excuse us now, Brother."

As I turned to leave he sat down at the table next to Philomena. So little time, so much to discuss.

IT WAS MY turn to give the reading at dinner. For my text, I chose Revelations, 6:

> *And there went out another horse that was red: and power was given to him that sat thereon to take peace from the earth, and that they should kill one another: and there was given unto him a great sword . . .*

I kept glancing up at Maraviglia as I read, which did not seem to amuse him.

When I finished, I took my seat next to the Abbot. Maraviglia stood and somberly walked to the lectern.

"Father Abbot, Brothers," he began, "I have a sad and painful announcement. My time with you is drawing to a finish."

The Abbot whispered, "A heavy cross, but we must bear it cheerfully."

"In the past months, many of you have wondered what it was that kept me so long here at Cana. . . ."

"Château Figeac," the Abbot muttered.

"The truth is, I was not simply doing an audit of the monastery's finances...."

"No," the Abbot continued, "you were also busy watching soccer on my TV."

"I think we should listen to this," I whispered back.

"A financial review is not complicated. That would require only a week, perhaps. No, Brothers, I was conducting a more important review—an audit of the soul of Cana."

The Abbot groaned. "Oh, *spare* me."

"And I found a soul in ruins." His eyes turned cold and reproachful. "You took vows to walk humbly in the footsteps of Christ, and I find you driving a Lexus...."

"I told you to hide the car!" the Abbot hissed.

"I did," I hissed back. "He must have found the receipt."

"You took vows to follow the teachings of Holy Scripture, and I find you reading someone named Deepak Chopra, M.D. You took vows not to worship false idols, and I find you building a *mountain* of them. Fountains of wine! Brambles that move by motor! You took vows to serve humanity, and I find you stealing from humanity.

"The Cardinal hoped that my presence here would cause you to reform. He hoped that you would once more renounce the ways of the world, and take up the way of Saint Thaddeus. And what happened? You committed the worst abomination of all. This, this"—he spat out the word—"*infomercial*. You have set the Catholic Church back five hundred years. The Holy Father himself viewed it."

The monks stirred.

"The Cardinal showed it to him this week. He was profoundly saddened. He asked His Eminence to come here himself, to take charge personally."

The Abbot said weakly, "Cardinal Blutschpiller? Is coming—here?"

"Yes. Next week. He will conduct the Papal Court of Inquiry. He will also attempt to negotiate with the civil authorities. If I were you, I would pray very hard for the Cardinal's successful intervention. Not only God's laws have been broken here. You can be imprisoned for the deceptions that you have inflicted on the public."

The Abbot slumped back in his seat.

"As we prayerfully await his arrival," Maraviglia continued, "the Cardinal has issued the following orders. First, we will tomorrow suspend all activities at the Pilgrims Center, including the Cask-Ade. Second, we will turn off the wine fountain. Third, we will remove the pile of crutches. Fourth, all Cana assets and accounts will be frozen immediately, pending the Cardinal's decision. Fifth, we will resume the monastic discipline as prescribed by Saint Thaddeus. You are not required to throw yourself onto thorn bushes, or to beat one another with goat bladders, but you will rid your cells of modern electronic devices and implements of leisure. I must tell you that I was surprised during my audit to find receipts for golf clubs. Sixth, no one will leave the monastery or communicate with the outside world without express permission from me. You will please immediately convey to me the keys to all vehicles." He glanced at the Abbot. "This includes the Lexus."

It was very still. Several dozen monks looked down at their plates.

"And now," said Monsignor Maraviglia, "let us all bow our heads and pray for Our Lord's forgiveness."

He opened our breviary and read from Saint Thad's "Prayer in Time of Tribulation." It wasn't reassuring to consider that these were the last recorded words of our patron before the Sultan tired of torturing him and sawed off his head:

> " 'Lord, look down on me, a wretch, and grant that my suffering be even greater than my sins. Let the pain wrack my limbs. And when that pain is done, unleash an even greater agony. And when I think the worst is over, surprise me with unimaginable torments, so that on Judgment Day, my sins shall be paid for, and all shall say, "Truly, this man knew pain." ' "

THE WEEKEND PASSED slowly. Forbidden to use my computer, I spent the time doing something I had not done in a long while—prayer and contemplation. Most of the other monks did the same. There was an unmistakable air of spirituality about Cana, but then, to paraphrase Dr. Johnson, nothing so concentrates the mind as the prospect of having your head sawed off on the morrow.

The Abbot said nothing at meals, and otherwise remained in his cell. Even our normally cheerful Brother Jerome seemed subdued. Only Brother Bob managed to lift our spirits. On Sunday morning as we filed out of chapel after Mass, he began whistling the tune of "It's a Long Way to Tipperary," and then softly singing, "Oh, it's a long way to Kis-an-gan-i. . . ."

At dinner he passed out photocopied pages of a list he had drawn up called "Useful Congo Lingo," as well as a practice dialogue called, *"Une conversation Kisanganaise entre Frère Jacques et Frère Jim."* The dialogue went as follows:

BROTHER JACQUES: Oo la la, how hot it is!

BROTHER JIM: Not as hot as the infernal region. Heh heh!

JACQUES: It is not the heat, so they say, but the humidity.

JIM: I implore to differ! Here we say, It is not the malaria but the leprosy.

JACQUES: Say, speaking of that, did you not have two hands when we met for breakfast?

JIM: Why, you are correct! Where is my left hand? Have you seen it?

JACQUES: Perhaps it is at the library. Shall we go and search for it together?

JIM: Good idea! But let us take our countermalaria pills first.

JACQUES: Of agreement! Or instead, we could simply drink some of the miracle wine of Cana. They say it cures everything. Maybe it would grow you a new extremity.

JIM: Please, I demand to you, speak to me no more of this cursed wine!

JACQUES: Exclaim! Here comes Brother Auguste.

JIM: Excuse me, Brother. Have you seen my left hand?

AUGUSTE: I regret, no. But now let me ask you—is this your sandal?

JIM: Certainly not! Where did you locate it?

AUGUSTE: Inside the enormous crocodile that the natives have captured. Tell me, have either of you seen Brother Anatole?

JACQUES: Not since yesterday afternoon. I saw him doing the wash yesterday afternoon, down by the river.

AUGUSTE: Sacred blue! That makes the third eaten monk this month! Whose turn is it now to do the wash? Attend! To where are you two running so quickly?

After dinner I went for a walk to clear my head. It was a lovely summer's evening. In the gathering twilight, there was a certain serenity and even majesty to Mount Cana— perhaps because there were no screaming pilgrims sliding down the flume, no mechanical brambles enticing them to throw quarters, no fountain bubbling with false promises.

I climbed the path up to the shrine of Saint Thad. I was standing in front of it, lost in thought, wondering how our patron saint would have dealt with our situation, when I was startled by a voice—Philomena's.

"Need a quarter?" she asked.

"Actually, yeah," I said. "The Monsignor took all mine."

"I don't have my purse, otherwise I'd lend you one."

"What, and go against the Monsignor's orders? You wouldn't do something like that."

"Ty," she said, "it's a nice night out. Could we have a nice conversation?"

"Why not," I said.

We sat down together on the bench next to the shrine.

"Quarter for your thoughts," she said. "And I won't tell Monsignor."

"Okay. I could use the money. Since you ask, I was re-hearsing some useful French phrases. For instance, *'Pardon, mademoiselle. Est-ce que tu a vu ma main gauche?'*"

"It's at the end of your wrist. What are you talking about."

"Leprosy jokes are all the rage right now in the calefac-tory. Never mind, you had to be there."

She sighed. "I guess you guys have a pretty gruesome week ahead."

"*You* guys? What do you mean? Seems to me that our marketing consultant had something to do with all this. Including this pile of—we're standing on. You've got some music to face, too."

"I know. I just meant, I'm not exactly a member of the order. What can Blutschpiller do to me? Defrock me? But you're right. I screwed up. I should have listened to you. Things just got *way* out of control here."

"Like the infomercial? *It's just a naive Chilean cabernet, but I think you'll be amused by its supernatural powers.*"

"You probably won't believe this, but I fought Brent tooth and nail on that one. Guess who overruled me every time."

"His Holiness Deepak Chopra."

"M.D. I even tried to shut down production one day. I shouted, 'Brent, you cannot have people throwing off their goddamn *crutches!*' The Abbot took me aside and explained that the pile of crutches was just a metaphor for 'the Field of all Possibilities.' Next day he gave me a personally inscribed copy of Deepak's *Ageless Body, Timeless Mind.*"

"I can't wait to hear him explain all that to the Great Excommunicator and the BATF. So, where do you think we'll all end up? The Congo, or Leavenworth?"

We laughed. It almost seemed like old times.

"Look," she said, "the moon."

"It's not full this time. I mean, tonight."

She touched my arm tenderly. "I know what you meant. That's what I was thinking too."

I looked into her eyes. They were still beautiful.

"Whatever happens," she said, "I just hope you can find it in your heart to forgive me."

"What do you mean?"

"Just don't blame it all on me."

"No," I said. "We were all in this together."

"Thanks, Ty." She leaned over and gave me a quick peck on the cheek. Then she got up quickly and hurried down the path back to the Pilgrims Center.

"Attend!" I called after her when she was out of sight. "To where are you running so quickly?"

THE NEXT MORNING, Monday, I looked for Maraviglia at Matins. I needed his permission to call the shipping agent to make sure that our wine was ready on the docks in Newark. I also needed to get cash from him to cover the truckers' "bonus" for rushing it to us.

He wasn't at prayers. When he didn't appear at breakfast I went to find him. There was no answer when I knocked on the door to the Executive Conference Center. I cautiously opened it.

"Monsignor?" I called. No answer. The rooms were empty. The bed didn't look slept in. As I stood there wondering where he could be, the terrible thought crossed my mind—did he spend the night with Philomena at the Pilgrims Center? Was *that* why she hurried off?

I didn't really want to know. I scribbled a note to the Monsignor about the wine and the bonus, and left.

When I hadn't heard anything by eleven, I decided I'd better go ahead and call the agent. He told me that the wine had cleared customs but still had not received authorization from the Chileans to release it. I called Chile and spoke with Señor Baeza at the winery.

"I regret, *Fray*," he said, using the Spanish word for friar, "but the funds have still not arrived in our account."

"Could you call your bank and speed the process? It really is important for us to get the wine immediately."

"Very well," he said, "but perhaps you should also call your bank. In our experience, the problem has been at your end."

I hung up and called Mr. Terens, who handled our account at the New York bank.

"Oh yes, Brother Ty," he said. "The transfer went through."

"I *knew* it," I said, annoyed. "It's sitting there on a desk in Santiago, underneath someone's *café con leche*."

"Not Santiago," said Mr. Terens. "You canceled the Santiago transfer."

"What?"

"Let me check. Here it is. I have Monsignor Maraviglia's fax of Friday at noon, authorizing a Monday-morning transfer of two million dollars to Banco Bolivar. Then another fax, dated Sunday at four P.M., instructing me to cancel that transfer and instead to wire...let's see, I know it was a large amount, just about everything in the account...yes, here it is, nine million, eight hundred thousand."

"Nine point eight mil—to Chile?"

"No, to the Grand Caymans. To the account at the Schweiner Bank of Zurich. Per Monsignor Maraviglia's instructions. He called this morning just after nine, to confirm."

I rushed back to the Executive Retreat Center. Still no sign of him. I ran and got the Abbot. Together, we returned to the suite and began looking around. The closet was empty, and there were no toiletries in the bathroom.

"The message light is blinking," said the Abbot, pointing to the answering machine on his old desk. He went over and pressed PLAY.

The first two messages were in Italian from the same person, judging from the gravelly voice. I could only make out the words *"urgente"*[36] and *"presto."*[37]

The third message was a woman's voice. "Yes, this is Air Canada calling for Mr. R. Mara... Maravig-glia, regarding Flight 987, scheduled for departure at 9:35 A.M. from Toronto. Please be advised that the flight has been delayed due to an equipment problem. It is now scheduled to depart Toronto at 11:50 A.M. If you have any questions, please call 800-776-3000."

The Abbot and I stared at each other for a moment. The digital clock on the answering machine read 12:36 P.M. We both reached for the phone at the same time. He turned on the speakerphone and dialed. A voice came on, telling us how important our call was to Air Canada. Two minutes later we got to ask a human being about Flight 987.

"Let's see," she said, "987 was delayed... it departed Toronto at... 12:05."

"Where—where'd it go?"

"Havana."

"Havana, *Cuba?*" said the Abbot.

"That is the only Havana we service, sir."

I hung up. We looked at each other. The Abbot said, "Oh my God."

[36] Italian: "urgent."
[37] Italian: "quickly."

"What?" I said.

"The wine!" He ran for the steps leading down to his wine cellar. I followed. The Abbot hurried up and down the rows, inspecting the gaps in the orderly rows of bottles protruding from the racks.

"Look at this!" he muttered. "The '82's—*gone.*" He rounded a corner. I heard a chilling cry.

"That bastard!"

"What is it?"

"He took *all* the '61 Romanée-Conti! I had five bottles here!"

"Father," I said, "I'm sorry about your wine, but we're also missing ten million dollars."

"Do you have any idea what a bottle of '61 Romanée-Conti goes for?"[38]

The Abbot appeared from around the corner, and stood in the catacomb-like gloom. He shook his head bitterly. "I guess the 'audit of Cana's soul' included stealing our best wine in addition to all our money."

"Let's find Philomena," I said. "See what she knows."

We went out the back door of the wine cellar and headed across the parking lot to the Pilgrims Center. It was then we noticed that something else was missing—the Lexus. "No wonder he wanted the keys," the Abbot said. When we reached the Pilgrims Center, we found something else missing.

Philomena.

I found the note on her desk. It was addressed to me:

---

[38] About $3,200.

Dear Ty,

 I have to get away. Please explain to the Abbot and the other Brothers.

 I'm sorry that I won't be here in your hour of need. Please try to understand.

 Last night meant a lot to me. I'm glad we had one more moment on the Mount, and no sermon this time.

Love,

Philomena

The Abbot read over my shoulder.

" 'Moment on the Mount'?" he said. "Do I need to hear your confession, Brother?"

"Not for anything that happened last night," I said, "but definitely for the sinfully angry thoughts I'm having right now." I imagined them together on the plane, sitting in first class, decanting the Abbot's Romanée-Conti, on their way to Havana and Lord knows where next, with our $10 million.

"I can't *believe* she ran off with our money," I said. "It's one thing to swoon over some matinée monsignor, but to rob her friends..."

"I bet she wasn't in on the heist," said the Abbot. "He probably didn't even tell her what he'd done. She just thought they were eloping."

"Forgive me, Father, for I find still myself hoping that Flight 987 will experience the most extreme possible 'equipment problem,' preferably over shark-infested waters."

"Forgiven," said the Abbot. "Didn't the good Monsignor tell us that sinners should welcome pain?"

As I thought back on Maraviglia's final lecture to us about our sinfulness, fairly blinding us with his righteousness, I finally grasped the real lesson that he had imparted to us. He had taken our money, our wine, our car, and our management consultant, but had left us one thing of value, the Sixth Law of Spiritual and Financial Growth:

VI.

HE WHO CASTS THE FIRST STONE USUALLY WINS.

Market Meditation
the Sixth

The Bible says, "Let he who is without sin cast the first stone."
But if the competition and I are both sinners, who goes first?
If God didn't want people throwing stones,
how come He left so many lying around?
Is it just possible that the pharaohs built the pyramids to get the
stones away from people who wanted to throw them?
(Hint: name one pharaoh who was killed by a thrown stone.)
If Goliath had had a stone, wouldn't he have chucked it at David?
Who had a better understanding of the Sixth
Law™—Saint Thad or the Sultan who sawed off his head?
How did he get to be the Sultan, anyway?
So what's the deal with Philomena and the Monsignor?
They say that people who live in glass houses shouldn't throw stones.
Fair enough, but do I live in a glass house?
Does the competition live in a glass house?
Face it—do I know anyone who lives in a glass house?
(Okay, besides that rich guy in Connecticut who had Philip
Johnson for an architect? Come to think of it, wouldn't
a better rule be: "People who live in glass houses
shouldn't walk around naked"?)
Who won at Pearl Harbor?

Amazing—the questions keep getting harder, but you just
keep getting better!

Now, get a case of good Chilean wine (Maipo Valley, if
possible, but any kind will do). Open a bottle and drink it

slowly. Between sips, take deep breaths, close your eyes, and meditate on all the people who have done bad things to you (unprovoked insults, lectures on your so-called shortcomings, job dismissals, adultery with your best friend, embezzlement of your life savings, etc.). Write their names down on a piece of paper. When you've finished the bottle, put the piece of paper with their names inside it. (You'll probably have to roll it up tightly. Take your time.)

Open a second bottle of the wine. Repeat the drinking and breathing exercises above—only this time, think of all the things you wish you'd done to the bad people. (Remember to pace yourself—the best part is yet to come!) Now write your name on a piece of paper and put it inside the second bottle.

Set these two "glass houses" in front of you. Now, take a big cinder block, the kind they use to build nonglass houses. Hold it up over your head and pretend you're the bad people inside the first house. Hurl it at you, inside the second house.

So, who won? *Ouch!*

Now, open a third bottle of wine. Drink it, as above. Take another piece of paper and write your name on it again. (If you're having a hard time, initials will do.) Insert the piece of paper inside the bottle. Take your time—and remember to roll it up first. That will make it easier.

Set your new "glass house" down beside the bottle with the bad people. Watch out for those shards! Oops! Better get a Band-Aid.

Bleeding stopped? Good. Okay, this time *you* "throw the first stone"! Hold the cinder block over your head and aim it at the first wine bottle. Remember all the awful things they did to you. Bombs away!

Missed it? Not to worry. You can always "take a Mulligan," and you were going to buy a new stereo, anyway. Better unplug it—that will make the sparks and smoke stop. While you're at it, put the pet in the bedroom until you've concluded the exercise.

Keep throwing until you hit the bottle. Now, see what happens when *you* throw the first stone? Remember what happened when *they* threw the first stone? Beginning to see a pattern?

Prayer of
the Proactive Sinner

*Almighty Lord, who castigated Thy people in page after page
of Holy Scripture, never hesitating to
smite them mightily with sneak attacks of floods, plagues, boils,
frogs, and other horrendous instruments of Thy wrath;
who ruined the lives of perfectly nice people like Thy servant Job,
and won every time, remaining on top,
still God, a world-class Survivor, grant that my aim be true and
swift, and that my path be strewn with
excellent projectiles, and that mine enemies shall never
know what hit them.*

CHAPTER THE SEVENTH

The Palermo Connection...
A Media Nightmare...
One Last Tip...
The Abbot Assembles
the Talent Bank...
A Remarkable Conclusion

HE ABBOT AND I RUSHED back to the monastery. I got onto my computer and did a fast review of the activity in all Cana's accounts since Maraviglia assumed control of them. It turned out that the missing $9.8 million was only his most recent "withdrawal." The good Monsignor had all along been quietly draining our Reserve Fund, our Hedge Fund, and—to the Abbot's horror—the Viticultural Research and Development Fund (more commonly known as the Figeac Fund). All told, his "audit" had cost us a little over $16 million. Thirteen million had been wired to the Swiss bank in the Cayman Islands; the remaining three had gone to the Banco di Palermo in Sicily. Our assets now totaled $195,000—a tenth of what we needed to get our wine off the docks in Newark.

"It seems to me," the Abbot said, "that Blutschpiller owes us sixteen mil." He dug out Maraviglia's business card.

We called the number at the Vatican and got a recording asking us to choose from a menu of languages. After we selected English, the following came over the speakerphone:

> *"Welcome to the Vatican Office of Internal Investigations. To expedite your call, select please among these choices:*
>
> *"To report a new heresy, digit one.*
>
> *"To report the recurrence of an old heresy, digit two.*
>
> *"To report someone in the Church who has questioned the Doctrine of Papal Infallibility, digit three.*
>
> *"To report a moral irregularity, digit four.*
>
> *"To report a financial irregularity, digit five.*
>
> *"If you feel that you have been unjustly denounced or excommunicated, please make your complaint in writing.*
>
> *"To report an unauthorized ordination of a woman priest, immediately digit zero—an inquisitor will be with you shortly.*
>
> *"For all other matters, please stay on the line. Your call is important to His Eminence, the Cardinal."*

The solemn Dies Irae from Mozart's *Requiem* began to play. The Abbot digited zero. Within seconds a voice answered, *"Ufficio dell' Investigazione Interna. Vuole Lei communicare un' ordinazione femminile?"*[39]

---

[39] Italian: "You wish to report a female ordination?"

"No," said the Abbot, "I wish to report a thieving Monsignor."

"That is a financial irregularity. I will transfer you."

"No!" cried the Abbot. "This is *molto importante!*[40] I must speak with Cardinal Blutschpiller. I am the Abbot of Cana Monastery, in the United States."

Pause. "His Eminence has not the time to speak with every . . . *abbot* who telephones."

The Abbot was only momentarily stymied. "Listen to me very carefully. I am calling to report that Monsignor Maraviglia has ordained twenty-six women, all of them practicing lesbians."

"Momento," said the voice.

The Abbot said, "That should get their attention."

Soon a German-accented voice came on. "This is Father Haffman speaking."

I recognized the last name. "Father Hans," I whispered. "Blutschpiller's personal secretary."

The Abbot whispered back, "You be *my* 'personal secretary.'"

"This is Brother Ty speaking, from the Monastery of Cana in the United States. Father Abbot wishes to speak with His Eminence, the Cardinal. It concerns an urgent matter involving Monsignor Raffaello Maraviglia—executive secretary to the Cardinal."

"Is the Monsignor all right?"

"I can't answer that, since he's no longer here."

"Not there? Where is he, then?"

---

[40] Italian: "Very important!"

"Somewhere between Toronto and Havana."

"Havana, *Cuba?*"

"Havana, Cuba."

"What is he doing in Cuba?"

"The Abbot has no idea. All he does know is that the Monsignor has stolen from us approximately—"

The Abbot nudged me and whispered, *"Twenty."*

"—a...considerable sum of money. Many millions of dollars. It is imperative that Father Abbot speak to Cardinal Blutschpiller."

"His Eminence is not available. If I could speak to the Abbot, perhaps I can look into it."

"Please hold for the Abbot," I said archly. The Abbot waited a moment before coming on.

"Good evening, Father. I am the Abbot of Cana."

"Yes. I recognize your voice."

"You do?"

"From the television commercial. The one with the crutches."

"Ah," said the Abbot. He quickly changed the subject. He explained the situation. Father Hans listened without comment until the Abbot mentioned the three million that had been wired to the bank in Sicily. He asked for the date of that transfer.

When the Abbot had finished our tale of woe, Father Hans asked, "Who knows this, outside of you?"

"No one," said the Abbot.

"You will say nothing of this, to anyone, of course. This office will conduct a full investigation. You will be contacted."

The Abbot cleared his throat. "Forgive me, Father, but I don't think I made myself clear. The situation is that we need our money back, *presto*. We are in an emergency here. At the very least, two million dollars must be wired to our wine supplier in Chile—*today*—or our monastery will be publicly disgraced."

"That is impossible," said Father Hans. "It will take weeks at least to conduct a thorough investigation."

"Father, if we don't have that money right away, federal policemen will come to our monastery on Friday and arrest us. The publicity would be very bad not only for us, but for the Cardinal—try as we might to protect him. I fear the authorities would very soon learn that the Cardinal's own executive secretary, his trusted aide, has stolen money from an order of poor, humble monks."

There was a long pause. "The Cardinal would wish to avoid a public scandal. I can tell you confidentially that His Eminence had certain concerns about the Monsignor. He was, I can also tell you, planning an unannounced visit to your monastery. Even the Monsignor was unaware of it."

"No," said the Abbot, "the Monsignor was very much aware that the Cardinal was coming this week. He told us so himself, on Friday. In fact, he took the occasion to lecture us about our own moral failures."

"Impossible," said Father Hans. "He did not hear about it from us. The Cardinal was very clear that his visit was a secret."

"Well obviously it *wasn't* a secret, and obviously, that is why he left. With our money. Which his supervisor is, of course, responsible for."

"I will do everything I can. Fax me immediately what documents you have, in particular the ones pertaining to the bank in Sicilia."

THE SIGNIFICANCE OF the Sicilian deposit became clear the next morning, Tuesday.

The Abbot and I were walking across the parking lot to the Pilgrims Center, which we had decided to reopen in order to keep some revenue flowing, when I noticed two men in dark suits leaning against a parked sedan. My first thought was that the Bureau of Alcohol, Tobacco and Firearms had decided to move up the Friday deadline. But as they approached us there seemed something distinctly non-government issue about them. Federal agents usually don't wear $600 Italian loafers.

"Excuse me, Father?" said one, wearing sunglasses.

"Yes," said the Abbot.

"You're the Abbot, right? From the commercial?" He had a New York accent.

"Yes," the Abbot brightened.

"Great commercial. My wife ordered a case—for her sciatica."

"Ah," said the Abbot, "now, don't worry, we're working on those orders right now. We had such a tremendous response. But I assure you, she'll be getting it very soon now."

"Thank you. I appreciate that. I'll tell her. But we didn't drive all the way up here to bother you about that. We're looking for Monsignor Maraviglia."

For a moment I thought they must have been sent by the Cardinal, but there also seemed to be something distinctly non–Vatican issue about them. They didn't look like plain-clothes Swiss Guards.

"May I ask—who *are* you?" said the Abbot.

"We have some personal business with the Monsignor." He extended his hand. "Johnny Corelli. This is my associate, Mr. Scarpatti. From Palermo. We're sorry to disturb you, but we haven't been able to reach the Monsignor. We really need to talk to him. Normally we don't go to a client's place of employment."

"Well, his 'place of employment' is really the Vatican, in Rome."

"*Non sta là,*" said Mr. Scarpatti. "Not there." I recognized the gravelly voice from the Monsignor's answering machine.

"What kind of business do you have with the Monsignor?" asked the Abbot.

"He owes Mr. Scarpatti some money."

"For what?"

Mr. Scarpatti said, "*Calcio.*"

"He liked to bet on soccer games," said Corelli. "Big bets."

"AC Milano," said Scarpatti. "His team. Not so many wins this year."

I spoke up. "I caught the end of the Stuttgart game."

Scarpatti rolled his eyes. "*Buffoni!*[41] For Milano, a disgrace. For the Monsignore—*puh!*"

"He kept losing, so he kept betting more. It happens," said Corelli.

"How much does he owe?" asked the Abbot.

"His number is four million dollars."

---

[41] Italian: "Buffoons!"

"Four *million*?" said the Abbot. "Why would you let a priest run up a tab like that?"

"He was a good client. From a good family. His father used to do business with Mr. Scarpatti's father. Pretty high up in the Vatican. Up to now, he always paid. He paid off three million a couple of months ago."

"By any chance," I ventured, "would that have been a wire transfer to the Bank of Palermo?"

"*Sì*," said Scarpatti.

"But that's *our* money!" said the Abbot.

So that is where our money is at the moment. I studied Scarpatti's impassive face and thought, *And where it is likely to stay.*

"Father," said Corelli, "it's not our business where the money comes from."

"Well, it's *our* business," said the Abbot. "And it's *our* money, and we need it back."

"Father," said Corelli, "I don't think we should waste time worrying about that money."

"Very well," said the Abbot, digging in his heels, "then I don't see any reason to waste time discussing the present whereabouts of Monsignor Maraviglia."

Just then, a dark van entered the parking lot and pulled next to us. Its side door slid open to reveal a burly man with a television camera on his shoulder. He jumped out onto the pavement, followed by the closest thing in America to Franz Cardinal Blutschpiller. In the next instant, I heard the famous voice say, "Mike Wallace, with *60 Minutes*. You've ignored all our phone calls and letters. I'd like to ask you about some serious criminal charges—"

Mike Wallace stopped in mid-ambush, a look of distinct terror on his face. Four beefy men had suddenly appeared from around the CBS van. To judge from the accessories in their hands, they were associates of Messrs. Corelli and Scarpatti. Wallace and his crew found themselves staring down the muzzles of imposing handguns and submachine guns. I suspected it was Wallace's first counter-ambush. For once, he seemed at a loss for words.

"It's okay, boys," Corelli said to his bodyguards. "It's Mike Wallace. From TV."

The bodyguards lowered their guns.

"*Mike*," said Corelli, "you really shouldn't sneak up on people like that. They might get the wrong idea." He grinned. "It's not very polite."

"I had some questions for the Abbot," said Wallace, a bit shakily.

"Does that give you the right to interrupt? The fathers and I were having a talk. How would you like it if *you* were having a talk with a priest and I jumped out of a van?"

Mafia to the left of me, *60 Minutes* to the right of me—exactly the quiet, contemplative life I had sought as a refuge from the outside world. I imagined Wallace's opening narration for his piece on us: *We were greeted at this unusual monastery by its Abbot, four heavily armed men, and a man identified by law enforcement officials as a capo, or captain, of the . . .*

"Gentlemen," said the Abbot. "Please. Mike, I'll be happy to answer all your questions in a minute. But Mr. Corelli *was* here first. He's one of the many devout pilgrims who come from all over to Cana. He's very anxious to get some of our wine for his wife, Mrs. Corelli, who suffers from sciatica. Of course, Mike, we make no health claims—"

"That's not what BATF—"

"Mike, please. All in good time. Let me finish with Mr. Corelli." With that, the Abbot escorted Corelli and Scarpatti to their cars, followed by the dutiful bodyguards. The Abbot and Corelli spoke intently for several minutes. I saw Corelli scribble on a piece of paper and hand it to the Abbot. As they got into their sedans the Abbot made a little sign of the cross as a farewell blessing.

He rejoined us, heartily slapping his hands together. "So many different kinds of pilgrims we get here—from all walks of life."

"Like the mob?" Wallace asked as the camera rolled.

The Abbot smiled beatifically. "It's not for us to judge, Mike. Did Our Lord turn anyone away? Our mission is to serve all who come here in search of solace—kings and beggars, saints and sinners—even journalists."

"Father, the Bureau of Alcohol, Tobacco and Firearms is investigating your monastery on some *very* serious charges. Passing off someone else's wine as your own. Taking people's money and not filling their orders. While making *blatantly* illegal claims that your wine *cures* diseases. How do you answer these charges? What's going on here?"

"Mike, you're asking *excellent* questions," said the Abbot, continuing to smile serenely. It struck me that I had seen that smile before, in a video the Abbot had shown us. It was the invincible smile of Deepak Chopra, M.D. "And we are *truly* happy to answer them. Mike, we *do* have a problem here at Cana. Since using your own medium of television to reach out to people with our message of hope, wholeness, and healing, we have been stunned at the response. So many people have called our toll-free number—that's 800-T-R-Y-

C-A-N-A—that our little monastery has been overwhelmed."

"Hold on, you're saying that—"

"Exactly! I'm saying that unless they pick up the phone
right now and dial 800-T-R-Y-C-A-N-A, it may be too late to
order some of our wonderful wine. There are just *so* many
people out there thirsting for a reasonably priced, full-
bodied wine that not only goes well with just about anything, but leaves you feeling—"

"Look, you're saying people have paid you and you still
haven't—"

"Exactly, Mike. I'm saying that the need is so great out
there for hope, wholeness, and healing that we few monks
are just *scrambling* to keep up with production. Now I'm
going to tell you something I probably shouldn't. We've
been told we're making a very big mistake."

"You mean—"

"*Exactly.* We've been told, again and again—*raise your
prices!* But we're not going to do that, Mike. If someone out
there who is in pain goes to the trouble of dialing 800-T-R-Y-
C-A-N-A—"

"*Cut,*" said Mike Wallace to his cameraman. "Turn it off.
Just"—he made a disgusted waving motion with his hands—
"turn it off."

The Abbot smiled at him. "*Exactly,* Mike."

"Look, Father, I didn't come here to shoot your next infomercial."

"Really? You were doing such a good job. You've got a future in this business. Will this be on soon, I hope?"

"As a matter of fact, our piece is scheduled for this Sunday."

I thought I saw, beneath the Abbot's serene façade, a momentary flicker of panic. But he smiled on valiantly. "Oh," he said, "good. That's ... good."

"We're going to present these charges, you know. I'm here to give you the chance to refute them. Can we turn the cameras back on?"

"Hold off a moment," said the Abbot. "Here's the situation. We've had some production problems. That's the main issue. The health stuff, the labeling, that's a matter of interpretation, and I'm confident BATF is going to end up dropping that, as long as we start shipping product on Friday. That's the deal. We've invited them to be here then. I'm inviting you. Come back, watch the bottles roll off the line, and I'll answer all your questions then." The beatific smile disappeared. "Obviously, Mike, you want to have *all* the facts before you rush onto the air with something that's going to offend a hundred million Catholics." The blissful smile returned. "Or our lawyers."

Wallace seemed to recognize a worthy adversary. He nodded. "Okay, Friday. What time?"

"We told the BATF noon. Shall we expect the pleasure of your company as well?"

"Exactly."

THE ABBOT AND I spent the balance of Tuesday doing what monks used to do—beg.

Either we were out of practice, or $2 million was a little too much to ask for. Señor Baeza at the winery was in no mood to listen to my pathetic plea for credit. *"Lo siento, Fray Ty,"* he said, "but with your history of payment difficulties, it is impossible. The wine cannot leave the docks until the money is wired to our account."

The Vatican was no more help. Father Hans told the frantic Abbot, "We are fully aware of your temporal considerations. Be assured that we are proceeding as expeditiously as is possible on this matter while observing the necessary protocols." The Abbot translated this: "We are not going to do anything anytime soon."

I got little sleep that night. After evening prayers I went to my office and fired up the computers. It was time to call Our Broker.

I turned on BREVNET, our special software program for correlating our daily breviary readings with global financial news. I clicked away into the small hours trying desperately to match a scriptural reading with a market development somewhere in the world, but to no avail. At 2:00 A.M., eyes bleary with fatigue, I launched BREVNET into DEEPSEARCH mode, widening the database. As the computer went to work I nodded off.

It was going on dawn when I was awoken by the sound of the bells of Notre Dame Cathedral coming from the computer, followed by a voice saying, "Hallelujah, hallelujah! We have a match!" (I had programmed BREVNET to announce its findings with a flourish.) I looked up at the screen.

BREVIARY TEXT
TODAY'S MATINS READING

AND JESUS WENT INTO THE TEMPLE, AND BEGAN
TO CAST OUT THEM THAT SOLD AND BOUGHT IN

THE TEMPLE, AND OVERTHREW THE TABLES OF THE
MONEY CHANGERS, AND THE *SEATS* OF THEM THAT
SOLD *DOVES.*

MARK 11:15

MATCHTEXT
LOMBARD RATEWATCH NEWSWIRE

BONN—SPECULATORS AT THE WORLD'S *MONEY EX-
CHANGES* ARE BRACING FOR A BUSY MORNING WHEN
THE GERMAN CENTRAL BANK MEETS ON THURSDAY.
TWO NEW MEMBERS WILL BE TAKING THEIR *SEATS*
ON THE BUNDESBANK—BOTH SELF-DESCRIBED
"MONETARIST *DOVES*" COMMITTED TO LOOSENING
THE MONEY SUPPLY AND ALLOWING THE GERMAN
CURRENCY TO WEAKEN AGAINST THE DOLLAR.
TRADERS ANTICIPATE HEAVY VOLUME IN DEUTSCHE
*MARK*S AT *11:15* A.M., WHEN AN ANNOUNCEMENT IS
DUE FROM THE BUNDESBANK MEETING.

I checked the markets and saw that currency speculators
were already betting that the deutsche mark would fall—the
so-called doves would carry the day. And yet the Gospel
reading for the day seemed to indicate that the currency
speculators, the world's "money changers," would have their
expectations dashed—the "doves" would be overthrown
when the Bundesbank met tomorrow morning.

It was all rather a lot to absorb at five in the morning. It
seemed too complicated, somehow. In the past, Our Broker
had given us simpler tips. But begging monks can't be

choosers when the Day of Judgment is only forty-eight hours away. I went to see the Abbot.

The Abbot studied the computer printout intently. He looked up excitedly.

"Currency…loosening the money supply—that's it! It's right there in *The Seven Spiritual Laws of Success*! Page 28! He rushed to the bookshelf and pulled it out. He read:

> *"The word affluence comes from the root word, 'affluere,'*
> *which means "to flow to." The word affluence means*
> *'to flow in abundance.' Money is really a symbol of the life*
> *energy we exchange….Another word for money is*
> *'currency,' which also reflects the flowing nature of*
> *energy.' "*

As usual, I had no idea what he was talking about. "Look, Father," I said, "I know this has been a stressful time for all of us, but I really think we need to stay focused."

"What could be more focused than *this*?" he said, giving the opened book an emphatic whack. "Don't you see? Deepak approves the breviary reading!"

"That must come as a great relief to Our Lord," I said. "Then you want to put all our money on the D-mark making a surprise rally tomorrow morning?"

The Abbot studied the printout one more time, his brow furrowed. "Yes," he finally said. "It's all…perfectly clear."

"I certainly hope so," I said. I went off to call Bill and told him to buy us D-mark calls.

"You've got a hundred and ninety-five and change left in the account," said Bill. "How much do you want?"

"Put it this way, we need it to turn into two million by tomorrow."

"Is your guy sure about this?"

"Yes," I sighed. "In fact, *both* our guys seem to agree."

"Jesus, you've got another one?" I heard him clicking away at his keyboard. "Okay, that's fifty-eight even calls at one point each . . . $195,000. You got it."

ONCE AGAIN, I didn't get much sleep. I awoke long before dawn on Thursday. Skipping Matins, I went to my office and paced nervously in front of my computers, waiting for the Bundesbank to issue its announcement. At 6:17 A.M. our time, the Reuters bulletin flashed on my monitor:

BUNDESBANK LOPS .25 OFF LOMBARD RATE
BONN—AS EXPECTED, THE GERMAN CENTRAL BANK
TODAY LOWERED ITS INTEREST RATE. THE QUARTER
POINT DROP ANNOUNCED AFTER THURSDAY'S MEET-
ING REPRESENTS A VICTORY FOR THE SO-CALLED
DOVES. . . .

I could read no further. Hoping against hope, I switched to another screen to see what had happened to the D-mark. Perhaps somehow, it would be soaring upward, defying the laws of economic gravity. Surely Our Broker and the wise Deepak Chopra, M.D., had power to give it flight.

But no, the laws of economic gravity were working just fine this morning. The D-mark was falling—and we with it.

I was still sitting numbly at my screen when the call came, and it was not Our Broker on the line. It was our broker, Bill, with the news that we were ruined.

"Well," he said, "I guess your guy is human after all."

"One of them certainly is," I said morosely. "So our calls are worthless."

"Yeah. Sorry."

"Do we have *anything* left?"

"Let me see... yes, well, not really. Three-oh-five."

"Three dollars and five cents?"

"No," said Bill, trying to be cheery. "Three hundred and five dollars."

THE ABBOT WAS reading to the monks at breakfast when I slunk into the refectory. He stopped in midsentence when he saw me.

"Do you have tidings, Brother Ty?" he asked. The monks turned to me expectantly.

"Yes, Father. I have good tidings, and bad tidings."

"Begin with the good."

"Looking at the long term," I said, "our portfolio has shown definite growth." It was a line I had often used on my distraught clients at the brokerage. "You'll recall that our initial portfolio three years ago when you entrusted me with Cana's assets was $304. As of this morning, it has grown to... $305."

"Well *done*, Brother," the Abbot gasped, gripping the lectern for support. "I suppose that takes care of your bad tidings as well."

I explained to the monks that we had lost our $195,000 on the deutsche mark.

"We were acting on guidance from our breviary, and," I said with a trace of huffiness, "from that international currency expert, Deepak Chopra, M.D."

"Hold on. Don't go blaming Deepak," the Abbot retorted. "He was merely encouraging us to invest in currency. It was your *breviary* that told us the mark was going to take off."

I started to protest, but the Abbot wearily waved me off. "Let us not point fingers, Brother. The question is not what happened. The question is, what next?"

"Kisangani," muttered Brother Bob.

"I heard that," said the Abbot. He reached into the folds of his cassock and took out his old, charred copy of *eating Affluence*. "This is no time to lose faith." He flipped it open and began to read:

> *"T stands for talent bank. In order to maximize creativity and offer the best service, it is good to develop a talent bank or a coterie of individuals with unique and diverse talents and abilities and whose individual talents, when added together, are more than the sum of the parts."*[42]

The Abbot looked up. "Look at the talent we have right here. Look at the resources in our own library, the finest of its kind ever assembled. This is the Alexandria of self-improvement literature. If the Lord helps those who help themselves, we cannot fail. Come, brothers! We have work to do!"

THREE HOURS LATER, we assembled around the mahogany table in the calefactory. The Abbot had ordered each monk to come up with an "action plan" derived from the work of a specific author. Now he called us to order.

---

[42] *Creating Affluence*, p. 52.

"Brothers, in less than twenty-four hours, the wine must begin flowing." He grinned with self-assurance. "It is not a question of *whether* we will do it, but *how* we will do it. The wine *will* flow—from wherever it is at the moment. All we need is a plan. Who will start?"

There were no volunteers, so the Abbot called on Brother Theo, our authority on *The Seven Habits of Highly Effective People*.

"Brother," said the Abbot, "you know that I am not a Coveyan, but let us rise above sectarianism. Bottom line—what do we do?"

Brother Theo rose to his feet and cleared his throat, "While I was not specifically able to find an 'action plan,' I'm confident that we can devise one, based on Covey's bedrock principles. This book has been on *The New York Times* best-seller list for more than five years. It contains invalu—"

"Brother," said the Abbot, "we have twenty-four hours. Get *on* with it."

"Very well. As I see it, all we have to do is follow the seven habits. One, 'Be Proactive.' Two, 'Begin with the End in Mind.' Three, 'Put First Things First.' Four, 'Think Win/ Win.' Five, 'Seek First to Understand, Then to Be Understood.' Six, 'Synergize.' Seven, 'Sharpen the Saw.' "

Brother Bob leaned over to me and said, "Isn't that what the Sultan said?"

"So . . ." continued Brother Theo. He cleared his throat again. "As I see it, we need to be proactive in understanding first . . . how to put the first case of wine at the end of a truck . . . in a synergizing . . ."

"Thank you, Brother Theo," said the Abbot. "Brother Alban?"

Brother Alban, our resident Napoleon Hill scholar, stood and held up a copy of *Think and Grow Rich*. "This book has been reprinted forty-two times, and read by over seven million *extremely effective* people," he said, giving Brother Theo a snide glance. "My text for today is from the section entitled 'Six Steps That Turn Desires into Gold':

> "*1. Fix in your mind the* exact *amount of money you desire.*
> "*2. Determine exactly what you intend to* give *in return for the money you desire.*
> "*3. Establish a definite date when you intend to* possess *the money you desire.*"

"How about twelve-twenty P.M.," said the Abbot, looking at his watch.

Brother Alban continued:

> "*4. Create a definite plan for carrying out your desires.*
> "*5. Write out a clear, concise statement of the amount of money you intend to acquire.*
> "*6. Read your written statement aloud twice daily, once just before retiring at night, and once after arising in the morning. As you read, see and feel and believe yourself already in possession of the money.*

"So," said Brother Alban, "I think what we should do is write out this statement and chant it tonight at prayers."

The Abbot rubbed his temples. "Brother Alban, why don't you write down the figure 'two million dollars' and fax it to the winery in Chile. Perhaps if *they* chant it, they'll believe they are already in possession of it."

On it went, each expert more useless than the last. There was nothing in *How to Win Friends and Influence People*, nothing in *Wealth Without Risk*, nothing in *Swim with the Sharks*, nothing in *Your Infinite Power to Be Rich*, nothing even in *Creating Money*.

Finally, the Abbot turned, with reluctance, to Brother Gene, his old Robbinite nemesis. "Well, Brother," he said sarcastically, "did you *Awaken the Giant Within?*"

"Might I remind Father Abbot," said Brother Gene, bristling, "that Anthony Robbins has advised some of the best minds in America—"

"Such as Leeza Gibbons and Ben Vereen—yes, Brother, we've seen the infomercial. But what does the giant have in mind for *us?*"

Brother Gene said, "Chapter Twenty-two. Financial Destiny: Small Steps to a Small (or Large) Fortune."

"Give me a Large," said the Abbot.

Brother Gene read:

> *"Let's review the five fundamental lessons*
> *for creating lasting wealth . . .*
> *" 1. The first key is the ability to earn more*
> *income than ever before, the ability to*
> *create wealth.*
> *" 2. The second key is to maintain your wealth.*
> *" 3. The third key is to increase your wealth.*

"4. The fourth key is to protect your wealth.
"5. The fifth key is to enjoy your wealth."

"Brother," said the Abbot, "I hear a sound. A loud, rumbling sound. The sound of the giant within—snoring. And his feet stink."

"Then tell us, Father Abbot—enlighten us. What does Deepak Chopra, M.D., have to say about getting our wine off the Newark docks?"

"Well," the Abbot sniffed, "I can at least do better than *that*." He thumbed through *eating Affluence*, then picked up *The Seven Spiritual Laws of Success*. "How about…hmmm… page forty-four… '*You can use the* Law of Karma *to create money and affluence, and the flow of all good things to you, anytime you want.'* Yes, and he's got an exercise at the end of the chapter." The Abbot found the exercise and read it.

" '*I will put the* Law of Karma *into effect by making a commitment to take the following steps: 1) Today I will witness the choices I make in each moment.… 2) Whenever I make a choice, I will ask myself two questions: "What are the consequences of this choice that I'm making?" and "Will this choice bring fulfillment and happiness to me and also to those affected by this choice?" ' "*

The Abbot stopped and reread it to himself. He continued, " '*3) I will then ask my heart for guidance and be guided by its message of comfort or discomfort. If the choice feels comfortable, I will plunge ahead with abandon.' "*

Solemnly the Abbot closed the book.

"That's helpful," Brother Gene said.

"It is," said the Abbot. "It is. My heart is comfortable with the choice I am about to make." He picked up his two books

and hurled them into the fireplace, rather violently. I
watched as the flames turned *eating Affluence* into

FLU

Deep   Opra

and then into ashes. His *Seven Spiritual Laws of Success* were
soon reduced to none.

"Is there a breviary in the house?" the Abbot asked. "You
know, the kind with the words of Our Savior in it?" I handed
him mine. He took it, opened it and read from Our Broker's
last stock tip, only this time he continued on, concluding
with Jesus' words after overturning the tables of the money
changers: " *'My house shall be called of all nations the house of
prayer, but ye have made it a den of thieves.'* "

With that, he picked up his end of the table and lifted it
so that all the books slid off the far end. One by one, the gods
of self-improvement landed with a thud on the marble floor.

LATER THAT AFTERNOON, after spending more fruitless
hours on the phone begging for money and wine, I went to
see the Abbot. I found him in, of all places, the winery, in the
upper vat room. It was the first interest he had shown in do-
mestic wine in ages. He looked remarkably calm, all things
considered.

"You know, Ty, that felt *great*. I had no idea book burning could be so satisfying. It gives me new insight into
Savonarola."[43]

---

[43] Fifteenth-century reformist Italian monk renowned for his "bonfires of the vanities,"
in which heretical books were put to the torch.

"You were in excellent form," I said. "What are you doing here?"

"I thought I'd see how much of this homemade swill of ours we have left." He peered over the rim of the tank of Cana wine that fed into the droplet-dispensing machine. "Uchh," he said. "Vintage Cana. Full-bodied, hints of rust, tetanus, and Tang. Weren't we going to do something about this?"

"We got sidetracked."

The Abbot checked the gauge. There was a little under 700 gallons.

"If we transfer this downstairs into the main tank," he said, "how long can we keep the production line going?"

"Maybe forty-five minutes."

The Abbot considered. "That might be long enough. How long can they watch bottles come off a line before getting bored?"

"Let's pray that BATF and *60 Minutes* have a short attention span. And that they don't ask for a taste."

"Oh, let them try it. It would solve our problems."

"How?"

"By poisoning them." The Abbot climbed down the ladder. We opened a valve, draining the wine into the downstairs tank. "So it's finally come to this," he said. "Bottling our own wine."

"Desperate times call for desperate measures."

"I'm still trying to pry the money out of that tightwad Hun. Father Hans keeps telling me they're working on it. I can see why it takes two hundred years to get someone canonized. I've told them Mike Wallace is coming, but it doesn't seem to carry much weight at the Vatican. I guess Mike hasn't ambush-interviewed the Pope lately."

"What about getting our Sicilian friends to lean on them," I suggested. "I'll bet the Holy See has heard of the Mafia."

"It's a thought," said the Abbot, wiping his hands. "I'll give Mr. Corelli a call."

DINNER WAS A glum affair. Even Brother Bob had no heart for Kisangani jokes. Only the Abbot seemed cheerful, or perhaps he was simply trying to keep our spirits up. After the last plate was cleared, he rose and went to the lectern.

"Brothers," he said, "I haven't given up trying to get our wine for tomorrow. But our prospects are, shall we say, uncertain. Cana needs a miracle. A real miracle. The kind we read about in the Bible. And this time, Brothers, we're going to go about it the old-fashioned way—we're going to *pray* for it."

"What's gotten into him?" Brother Bob whispered.

The Abbot announced that we would hold a vigil tonight at the foot of Mount Cana. "A candlelight vigil," he elaborated, "only brighter, and more warming." On his instructions we carted the contents of our self-improvement library into the courtyard, where we made a large pile. The Abbot, using his aspergillum,[44] sprinkled lighter fluid over it. Brother Jerome opened a case of Figeac—Maraviglia had not been able to take it all—and poured glasses for everyone. Then the Abbot lit a match and dropped it onto the pile. As the flames roared up, he lifted his glass.

---

[44] An instrument for sprinkling holy water.

"Brothers of Cana, I give you the Bonfire of the Inanities!"

We all gave a cheer. Brother Gene walked over to the Abbot, held out his copy of *Awaken the Giant Within*, and tossed it in. "That'll wake him up, once and for all." Brother Theo tossed in *The Seven Habits*. The former theological rivals embraced.

We stood around the warming fire, glasses in hand, chanting our evensong. There was a strange contentment in the air. Perhaps we were experiencing the inner peace the old martyrs felt on the eve of their executions. But then it could have been the Figeac.

OUR VISITORS ARRIVED just before noon the next day, which had become known around Cana as Bad Friday.

The Abbot was his most cordial self. "*60 Minutes,* may I introduce Bureau of Alcohol, Tobacco and Firearms. BATF, may I introduce *60 Minutes.* And now, ladies and gentlemen, if you'll follow me."

Mike Wallace sniffed the air as we walked to the winery. "Did you have a fire?"

The Abbot winked. "Just burned a few heretics at the stake last night. We're very old-fashioned here."

60 Minutes promptly switched on its camera. The Abbot promptly switched into his TV mode. "A fine day to be going about the Lord's work," he said, waving expansively at a busload of arriving pilgrims. "God bless you! God bless you!" As we passed by the foot of Mount Cana, he shouted up at another group. "That's it!" he cried. "Climb every mountain!" He began singing the song from *The Sound of*

Music. When he got to the part about following every rainbow, it was more than Mike Wallace could bear.

"I understand you're being sued by a pilgrim who was severely lacerated on your mountain," he said.

"*Who* can understand the workings of God's majestic grace?" the Abbot replied. "And here is our Grotto of Celestial Solace, where so many pilgrims lay down their burdens—"

"Where are the crutches?" Wallace demanded.

"Should pilgrims choose to leave behind personal effects like crutches, or wheelchairs, or canes, eyeglasses, respirators—which, Mike, we in no way encourage them to do—we donate these items to charities. We make no claim that our wine heals physical ailments." He nodded at the two stern-looking federal agents. "That would be illegal. Of course, this is a free country, and if people *say* they've been cured of terrible illnesses by our wine, we can hardly stop them. Ah, here we are, at the heart of Cana—our winery."

We entered the ground-floor bottling room. Dozens of monks were standing around in their work aprons.

"So why isn't the equipment running?" Wallace asked.

The Abbot replied with an air of surprise, "Why, Mr. Wallace, it is noon—a sacred hour for the Order of Saint Thaddeus. It was at noon that our founder experienced his penultimate mortification. He was standing outside a house of ill repute in Aleppo, denouncing the sinfulness within."

"And?"

"It turned out the Sultan was within."

The Abbot bowed his head and said, "Let us pray." The monks all bowed their heads. The Abbot began reading out

loud in Latin from the breviary. He finished the noon reading and kept right on going through the readings for the next
three weeks, eating up as much time as he could. The feds
and *60 Minutes* were getting visibly impatient—exactly as
the Abbot wanted them to be. Finally, he closed his book and
said, "Come, Brothers, we have wine to make."

He motioned to Brother Alban, who pressed the buttons
that started the machinery. Bottles of Cana wine began
coming off the conveyor. The Abbot grabbed the first bottle
and held it up proudly for the camera. "You know," he said,
"as long as we've been doing this, each bottle still seems like
its own little miracle to me."

"Where does this wine come from, Father Abbot?" Wallace asked. "We've learned that it's not even your own wine."

The Abbot managed a look of genuine sadness and shook
his head. "Mike, I know it's hard for some people, especially
our competitors, to believe that wine this good could come
from a humble monastery like ours. But I can *promise* you
that every drop of the wine in this bottle was grown, aged,
and bottled right here at the monastery of Cana."

"Could we have a taste?" Mike Wallace asked.

The Abbot hesitated. "Mike, you're putting me in a
slightly awkward position. As you know, there's a waiting list
a mile long for our wine. This bottle really should go to
someone who cared enough to call 800-TRY-CANA. But our
founder, Saint Thad, taught us that hospitality is next to
godliness, so I can hardly refuse."

The Abbot uncorked the bottle and poured two glasses.
He made a show of swirling the wine around inside the
glass, inspecting for "legs," and other signs of quality. When

he could postpone the fatal moment no longer, he took some in his mouth. It was a magnificent performance. He took the liquid in his mouth, closed his eyes with a convincing display of pleasure, and then heroically swallowed.

"Umm," he said. "Now, that's what I'd call ... wine."

Mike Wallace took a sip from his glass, and began choking. He turned around and spat it out as discreetly as he could. "Oh my—ach. What is that?"

"Assertive, isn't it?" said the Abbot brightly. "That's the Cana Nouveau. I myself love the robust, right-out-of-the-bottle flavor, but untrained palates might prefer to let it breathe."

"I'd give it a couple of years," said Wallace. He picked a large piece of orange grit from his teeth. "What *is* that?"

"Now, Mike," said the Abbot, "as I told Diane Sawyer, you can't expect us to give away our trade secrets."

Mike grilled the Abbot, who performed beautifully, managing not only to finesse the questions, but also to insert 800-T-R-Y-C-A-N-A into the middle of every potentially poisonous sound bite.

Finally the Abbot glanced at his watch—a half hour had gone by—and said, "One-fifteen. Where *does* the time go? I promised His Eminence the Cardinal I'd call him before he left for Castel Gandolfo. But I guess we've covered everything. May I show you gentlemen out?"

But the gentlemen from BATF were in no mood to leave just yet. They were keeping track of the bottles coming off the line.

"You've got thousands of cases to fill, Father," said the senior BATF agent. "We'll stay. But don't let us hold you up.

Go ahead and make your phone call." He grinned. "We'll be fine."

"So will we," said Wallace's producer.

"As you wish," said the Abbot, sounding unconcerned. "Then if you'll excuse me, I'll leave you in the good hands of Brothers Ty and Mike."

As I watched the Abbot withdraw I had to admire his calm in the face of impending doom. He seemed a true follower of Saint Thad. As for myself, I was sweating profusely. Any moment now, we were going to run out of wine, and I didn't want to be in front of *60 Minutes*'s camera when it happened. I asked Brother Mike to look after our visitors and excused myself.

"I promised Brother Theo I'd give him a hand with the filters," I said.

I walked to the back of the bottling room and opened the door into the filtering room. A dozen monks were gathered around the main tank, staring glumly at a vertical glass tube attached to its side. It was a gauge running from the top of the tank to the bottom, indicating the level of liquid within. I looked at the orangy-red column of wine in the tube. It was down below a quarter tank, and falling.

"We're almost out," said Brother Bob, flipping through his breviary in apparent search of inspiration. "Anyone up for hearing Saint Thad's final words again?"

"Please, anything but that," I said. I took out my own breviary and opened it, looking for something else appropriate to our dolorous situation, when—lo and behold, I came across an all too familiar passage. I had to smile.

"Okay, listen up," I said. I began reading:

"And the third day there was a marriage in Cana of
Galilee; and the mother of Jesus was there with Jesus
and His disciples.

   "And when they had drunk all the wine, Mary the
mother of Jesus said unto Him, 'They have no wine.'

   "And there were set there six water-pots, containing
two or three firkins apiece.

   "And Jesus said unto the servants, 'Fill the pots with
water.' And they did."

"Look—the gauge!" said Brother Benedict. "It's stopped
falling!" We looked up from our orisons. Sure enough, the
level in the glass column seemed to have stopped at the one-
eighth-full mark.

"Have they shut down the line?" Brother Bob asked. But
we could hear the sound of the bottles rattling along the
conveyor in the next room.

"Keep reading!" said Brother Benedict.

Not sure what was going on, I continued:

   "Jesus said, 'Now take some and give it to the chief steward.
The steward tasted it, but he knew not whence it came.'

   "The steward called over the host, and said unto him,
'Every man sets out at the beginning of a feast his good
wine, and then, when everyone has well drunk, that which
is worse. But thou hast saved the good wine until now.'"

"It's rising!" shouted Brother Bob. "It's rising!"

We stared in wonderment: the level was going up. It
passed the quarter-full mark, then the half-full mark, and
kept rising. No one spoke. One by one, the monks made the

sign of the cross and dropped to their knees, folding their hands in prayer, their eyes fixed on the amazing sight. Tears streamed down the cheeks of Brother Alban. He kept whispering the word *"Miraculum...miraculum..."* Even the color of the wine seemed to be changing. At last, Cana's wine took on a deep, rich, wine-dark hue.

I LEFT THEM there praying and rushed out to tell the Abbot.

The *60 Minutes* crew and the BATF agents were still observing the bottles coming off the line. Now I didn't have to fake heartiness. "Enjoying yourselves, fellas? Stay as long as you like. There's plenty more wine where that came from. If you need anything, Brother Mike will take care of you."

I was about to walk out the winery door when I realized that Brother Mike wasn't there to keep an eye on them.

"Where is Brother Mike?" I asked.

"He rushed off a minute ago," said the *60 Minutes* producer.

As I rounded the corner of the winery, I noticed Brother Mike at the top of the steel staircase leading to the upper vat room. He had a crowbar in his hand and appeared to be trying to jimmy the door.

I ran up the stairs. "Is there a problem, Brother?"

Brother Mike responded in his clipped tones, "Oh yeah. *Major* problem." He gave the crowbar a heave, cracking open the locked door. Whereupon he hoisted up his cassock and produced a black pistol from an ankle holster.

"Federal agent!" he shouted at the door, giving it a good kick.

The door burst open. There inside was the Abbot, standing on the ladder over the vat. In one hand was a plastic bucket from the Cask-Ade filled with Cana Red dye. In the other was a thick hose, which he was using to fill the vat with—water.

I gazed in horror. "*Ecce homo,*"[45] I said. "Our Lord's first miracle on earth was to turn water into wine. Yours is to turn wine into water."

"Brother" Mike was now flashing a shiny badge that said BUREAU OF ALCOHOL, TOBACCO AND FIREARMS.

"Special Agent Spodak," he announced. "You're under arrest for fraud." He put away his pistol, and motioned for the Abbot to extend his hands, which he then handcuffed. "Sorry, Father." He didn't apologize for cuffing mine. He pulled out a walkie-talkie and said into it, "Uncle One, move in."

He walked us down the stairs and back to the bottling room, where he handed us over to his BATF colleagues. The *60 Minutes* cameraman scrambled to get rare footage of monks in handcuffs.

As they marched us outside, Brother Jerome came running toward us.

"Another miracle!" he shouted. "The grapevines are walking!"

We looked toward the vineyard. Sure enough, some of the green vines appeared to be moving down the hill toward us. Then in the distance we heard the *whop-whop-whop* of helicopters approaching. In the next instant, several vans pulled up in front of us. The back doors flew open, and SWAT teams clambered out, guns at the ready, to take their

---

[45] Latin: "Behold the man."

positions. Now the helicopters were above, kicking up dust, and sending our cassocks up above our waists, like Marilyn Monroe's skirts over the subway grating. *60 Minutes* was in heaven.

"Is this *absolutely* necessary?" the Abbot shouted at the BATF people above the roar of the helicopters, as he tried modestly to push his cassock down with cuffed hands. "Were you expecting armed resistance, for heaven's sake?"

The senior BATF man motioned "Brother" Mike to take off our handcuffs. He waved off the helicopters, which began circling Mount Cana, causing pilgrims to scatter. "Religious cult in a heavily fortified environment," he explained to the Abbot. "Standard procedure since Waco."

"Gotta follow the regs," said Special Agent Mike. "Hey, they would've sent in tanks and APCs[46] if I hadn't talked them out of it."

"God *bless* you, my son," said the Abbot through clenched teeth.

"All right, let's round 'em up," said the senior BATF man. Special Agent Mike suggested they use the Executive Retreat Center as a "holding pen." Under the drawn guns of the centurions, we made our way along our Via Dolorosa.[47] BATF agents with megaphones were barking at the pilgrims, "Clear the mountain! This is a crime scene! Return to your buses immediately!" The confused and harried pilgrims, clutching their souvenir firkins, stared at our odd procession. It was all quite mortifying. Saint Thad would have loved it.

[46] Armored personnel carriers.
[47] In Jerusalem, the route Jesus took with His Cross to Calvary.

They took us to the Executive Research Center. More monks arrived in custody. The ones who had been working in the fields were accompanied by agents camouflaged with grapevines. Once they had assembled us all, the senior agent stepped forward and began, "You have the right the remain silent—"

"We *know* that," said the Abbot. "We're monks."

The agent finished reading us our rights. He said to Special Agent Mike, "Do a head count and let's get 'em out of here."

"Excuse me," said the Abbot. "May I say something?"

The senior agent nodded.

"There's no call to arrest all of us. This was all my fault. I accept full responsibility for any crimes committed here." Several of the BATF agents took out notepads and began scribbling.

"*Careful,* Father," I whispered. But he ignored me and kept going.

"I am the shepherd, this is my flock. I led them astray. Whatever they did, they did because I ordered them to. I was seduced by the writings of false prophets, and the promise of easy profits. And by the time I came to my senses, it was too late. We ourselves had been duped and lost our money. Believe me, we were going to fulfill those orders with real wine. We just needed a little more time. The purple dye was just for your benefit. We wouldn't have shipped those bottles. But I know that Caesar's laws have been broken, and someone has to pay. I'm your man. These are good monks. If they committed any crime, it was to believe in me."

The BATF agents huddled. They motioned over Special Agent Mike. I watched him nodding. The senior agent

turned to the Abbot. "Are you willing to sign a sworn statement to that effect?"

"Yes," the Abbot said.

Special Agent Mike helped one of the agents type it up
on the Abbot's own computer. The Abbot read it over and
signed it, adding a handwritten *"Mea culpa."* Then he asked
the senior agent, "May I have a few moments alone with my
monks to say good-bye? We'd like to recite the prayer our
founder said before he went to his fate at the hands of the
civil authorities."

The senior agent said, "Okay." The BATF left us to ourselves.

The Abbot headed for his bedroom. "Ty, a word."

I followed him in. He began changing into his civvies,
khakis and jacket.

"I guess you don't want to go to jail wearing a cassock," I
said, feeling sad. He crouched down and opened a cabinet.
Inside was a small safe. He twirled the dial, opened it and re-
moved a wallet, passport, and stacks of $100 bills.

"The Abbot's *own* hedge fund," he muttered.

"Will you be needing that in jail?" I asked.

"Ty," he said, continuing to stuff things into a small duffel. "I want you to hear my confession."

"But I'm not a priest," I said. "I'm only a brother. I can't
hear a confession."

"You can in an emergency," he said. He made a quick sign
of the cross and said, "Bless me, Brother, for I have sinned,
and I haven't finished. This being a confession, you cannot
reveal anything I'm telling you, so you are under no obliga-
tion to tell the authorities. You are therefore not an accessory."

"Accessory to what?"

"I'm not going to jail."

"You're not?"

"No. I'm going to make sure someone *else* goes to jail. I'm going to find that firking Monsignor, wherever he is, and read him a prayer of pain." He zipped up his duffel. "For these and all my sins I am most heartily sorry."

"But, Father—"

"Don't try to talk me out of it, Ty. Just give me my penance. On second thought, don't bother. I did my penance drinking that awful glass of Cana." He made a face.

I followed him out of the bedroom into the conference area. He addressed the monks. "Brothers, I pray you find it in your hearts to forgive your Abbot. Somewhere in the Field of all Possibilities, I got good and lost. Being Abbot of Cana was a great privilege that I did not live up to. But I promise you that I will strive with all my strength to atone for my sins. I leave you now in the good hands of Brother Ty. Now, Brothers, let us bow our heads as he leads us in prayer."

As I began reciting from *De Doloribus Extremis,* the Abbot patted me on the shoulder and, unseen by the others, disappeared down the steps into his wine cellar.

I KEPT THE prayers going as long as I could. Finally, after I had ignored the BATF's knocking on the door, it opened. Special Agent Mike entered.

"Come on," he said, "I know the prayer isn't *this* long. I did coverage on it." He scanned the room. Not seeing the Abbot, he searched the bedroom, bathroom, and multimedia room. "Okay," he said. "Where is he?"

"He said he wanted one last glass of good wine," I replied. "He went down into the cellar."

Special Agent Mike stood at the head of the stairwell and called down, "Father, time to go. No more wine. Father!" He went down the stairs. A minute later he came running up the stairs, with his walkie-talkie out.

"Uncle One. Big Daddy is on the run. Looks like he went out the rear door of the wine cellar. Seal the area."

He looked at us. "When did he split? How long?"

Brother Jerome asked innocently, "Father Abbot is gone?"

Special Agent Mike stared at him. "You didn't know?" He looked around at the perplexed faces. "All right, Brothers. Let's say you didn't know. But no one else leaves. Who's got a key to the back door of the cellar?"

I went down with him and unlocked it. He rushed out into the parking lot, already swarming with BATF agents. They were boarding tour buses full of departing pilgrims, looking for an abbot.

I was standing in the cellar doorway, taking in the strange scene, when I saw her standing in front of the Pilgrims Center.

AT FIRST I thought I must be hallucinating. It *had* been a stressful day. But then she saw me and started waving. She crossed the chaotic parking lot and came up to me.

"What are they all doing here?" she said.

"What are *you* doing here? I thought you were in Cuba. Or the Caymans by now."

"What?"

"You and Monsignor Marvelous, and our $16 million dollars."

"What are you talking about?"

"You didn't know? He stole all our money."

"Ohh," she said. "No wonder you called in the cops."

"No, the cops are looking for the Abbot."

"The *Abbot?*" Philomena shook her head. "I leave you boys alone for four days, and I come back to find the place under military siege." She started laughing. "Maybe we should have built that moat after all."

I gave her a brief account of our last week.

"I still don't get the part about me and Cuba," she said. "Why would you think I'd run off with a priest?"

"What did you expect us to think? He's gone, you're gone. You leave a cryptic note asking forgiveness. And let's face it, he *does* look like Richard Chamberlain."

"I just needed to get away. Maraviglia had shut down the Pilgrims Center. I needed to go someplace I could think. Preferably not a monastery full of hustlers."

"I see your point. So, where did you go?"

"Just up the road. I made a retreat at the convent." She looked down shyly for a moment. "I made a decision. I'm becoming a nun."

It took me a few moments to regain my power of speech. I stood there in shock, then I reached out and put my arms around her.

WE WERE STILL hugging tightly when two BATF agents went by and stopped to look at us.

"Some monastery they got here," one said to the other.

We ducked inside the wine cellar. There on the table was an open bottle of Figeac—the Abbot must have stopped on his way out for one last snort. We poured two glasses to celebrate Philomena's new vocation.

We talked about my last stock tip. "I can understand why it was a bad idea to follow Deepak's advice," I said. "What I don't understand is how our breviary went wrong. It was pretty definite about the money changers and the doves." I showed her the passage. She studied it.

"The breviary didn't go wrong," she said. "You just read it wrong. The money changers did get overturned—*you* guys were the money changers."

"Okay," I said, "but what about the doves?"

"You were the doves, too. The most common kind of dove is the pigeon. You were pigeons to fall for all those books. Only a sucker would believe those get-rich gurus. Why would anyone who knew the secret to easy wealth give it away for $9.95?"

She was right, of course. Once again, our breviary had provided timeless wisdom. There in the Abbot's wine cellar, I learned the Seventh Law of Spiritual and Financial Growth:

VII.

THE ONLY WAY TO GET RICH FROM A GET-RICH BOOK IS TO WRITE ONE.

Market Meditation
the Seventh

How many people do I know who read get-rich books?
How many of them got rich?
So where's Maraviglia now?
Did Saint Thad know the Sultan was inside the bordello?

Frankly, you've asked better questions. But this has been a trying day for all of us.

Don't be discouraged. You've still got what it takes. In fact, you're a beautiful person.

Okay, it's exercise time. Let's first warm up. Go to the bookshelves and take down every book offering a quick path to riches, power, sex, and valet parking. Now check the cover of each book. Does it mention sales figures? For example, "INSTANT INTERGALACTIC BEST-SELLER! OVER 4 MILLION COPIES SOLD!" Figure the author gets about $3 a book. Take out a piece of paper. Now, make two columns. In the left, write down how much the author made from the book. (For example, "$12 million.") In the right column, write down how much you've made as a result of the book. (For example, "minus $9.95.")

Repeat the process for every book. Then total both columns. If your total profits are greater than their total profits—but, hey, who are you trying to kid?

If the authors' profits are greater than yours by, say, a factor of five billion to one, then what lesson can we draw? (Hint: think "pigeon!")

Don't panic. There's still hope. We still have one more
law coming up—and we've saved the best for last!

Prayer of
the True Self-Helper

*Lord, who guided Thy people through the valley
of the shadow of death, guide me as I walk
through the aisle of the Personal Improvement
section of the bookstore. Grant that I might
see which self is, truly, helped by each of these books, so that
whatever I make by the sweat of my brow
might remain in my own pocket, and let me stand firm
against those who would have me be proactive.
Grant, further, that I might grasp the great wisdom that
awaiteth me at the conclusion of the next
and final chapter.*

CHAPTER THE SEVENTH AND A HALF

A Letter from the Abbot...
A New Mission for Cana...
The Last and Greatest Law

ANA WAS THE LEAD STORY on *60 Minutes* that Sunday. Since the Abbot was now an international fugitive, the focus was on him. They did a video montage of his monastic career—from the wedding commercial to the flume ride with Sebastian the Ghost to the handcuffs. I winced when they showed him telling Hugh O'Toole about "a secret ingredient we call love" and then immediately cut to a BATF agent carrying the plastic bucket of Cana Red dye, now labeled EVIDENCE. Diligent as ever, *60 Minutes* interviewed Señor Baeza at his vineyard in the Maipo Valley, and tracked down some thoroughly dissatisfied customers, including one woman who had broken her hip after drunkenly throwing away her walker.

"The BATF has shut down Cana winery," Wallace announced. A picture of the Abbot underneath the word WANTED flashed on the screen behind Wallace. I thought I caught Wallace smiling as he concluded his report: "As to the whereabouts of this *unusual* monk, it appears that for the time being, only *God* knows."

The BATF eventually established that the Abbot had sneaked onto a tour bus chartered by the Montreal chapter of the Society of Saint Blaise. One report had him boarding a train for Toronto. A month later, someone resembling him was spotted asking questions of the bar man at the Princess Hotel on Grand Cayman Island—where someone resembling Monsignor Maraviglia had stayed the week before. After that, the trail went cold.

The *60 Minutes* segment galvanized Father Hans. We struck a deal with the Vatican: if they would refund all the unfulfilled wine orders, we wouldn't tell anyone about their thieving Monsignor. The refunds got the BATF off our case. I made Father Hans put it in writing that we monks would remain at Cana, and not be sent "to do the Lord's work in any non–mutually agreed-upon location, specifically including Kisangani or any other community on the Congo River."

Our debts were paid off, but we were now back to an old, familiar situation—no money in the bank and no visible means of support. Should we go back into the wine business? We certainly had brand-name recognition—that was the good news. It was also the bad news. As the newly elected Abbot of Cana, I had to plot the monastery's future, if it had one.

I was sitting at my desk one day studying a catalogue of wine-making equipment when Brother Jerome came running in with a letter.

"The handwriting!" he said excitedly.

I recognized it instantly. The letter was postmarked Caracas. I opened it and read:

> *Dear Brother,*
>
> *I hope this letter has reached you, and not some trouble-some government snoop. If the latter, don't waste your time dispatching helicopters to Venezuela. I will be long gone.*
>
> *Sorry to have left in such a hurry. I was heartened to see the article in the Herald Trib saying the BATF had settled with you. I hear from certain Sicilian friends that you got Father Hans to cough up part of what was stolen from us. Bene! They told me also that they have been paid the balance of what was owed them. That still leaves plenty in the pocket of that Figeac-filching, soccer-betting ecclesiastical embezzler, and I aim to get it back before he blows it all. When I catch up with him, it will be my turn to read him Saint Thad's final words. I guarantee you, when I'm through with Monsignor M, all shall say, "Truly, this man knew pain."*
>
> *I've been thinking about you all. Are you planning a new line of wine? I'm no one to be giving advice, but here it is, anyway. Get out of the wine biz. Also, forget the other*

monk stuff—making cheese, jams, cakes, etc. Become a
postindustrial *monastery. Get back to the core mission of*
religion: retailing spiritual motivation. It's not about self-
*help—it's about self-*hope. *Get back to the core mission of*
the monastery, preserving and disseminating eternal wis-
dom. Cut out your overhead—throw out those rusty
vats—and give the people what they really want (aside
from good wine at reasonable prices). Bottom line: sell the
solace, not the sauvignon.

Have to go now. Am headed to a soccer match that
might turn out to be very interesting.

God bless you all, and remember to save the best for last.

Yr (former) Abbot

I took the letter up the road to Philomena, now doing her novitiate at the convent. We met in the visiting room.

"The Abbot seems pretty determined to get his hands on Monsignor Marvelous," I said. "I'd love to be there when it happens."

"Me too."

"I can see how someone could get in over his head with gambling. It's a disease. Maybe he got it from his father. What I don't understand is why he took all our money."

"I think he tried to pretend money wasn't important," she said, "but it was. He grew up rich, then his father lost it all. That's why he went into the Vatican—it was the closest thing to being rich again. But he hated Blutschpiller. He was *thrilled* to be away from him. Why do you think he spent so much time with us? That day he found out from you that Blutschpiller was on his way, he was devastated."

"So which of Saint Thad's mortifications do you think the Abbot has in mind for him?"

"He's probably going to start with sawing off his head," said Philomena.

"I wish him luck. But I don't know about the rest of the ideas in his letter. What does this mean, 'Sell the solace, not the sauvignon'? Sounds like warmed-over Deepak. Why can't we just make decent wine?"

"Ty," she said, "*forget* wine." She looked at the letter. "I like this 'postindustrial monastery' line. The bit about 'core mission.' I think he's on to something about low overhead. The Church used to sell indulgences, giving people time off Purgatory in exchange for cash. Now, *that's* low overhead."

"Well, if I decide to start selling indulgences, I'll be sure to hire you and Brent to do the infomercial. *Hold on, Sebastian. Are you saying that the next fifty callers will get a thousand days off their sentence in Purgatory—for the incredibly low price of just $19.95? And they'll get this handsome beach cooler at no extra cost?* Indulgences weren't the high point of Church history. There was something called the Reformation. I like to think that money isn't what the Church is all about. Monks *do* take vows of poverty."

"Hey," she said, "preaching about the evils of money is easy to do when you're a single male without a family to support. It sure made for a convenient message back when monasteries depended on donations from nobles trying to keep peasants from coveting their riches. Let's face it, money matters. Why shouldn't people want money?"

"Oh, I get it. The Sermon on the Mount just had it slightly wrong. What Jesus really meant was 'Blessed are the money-grubbers, for they shall drive imported cars.' You don't believe that. You wouldn't be here in a convent if you did."

"No," she said patiently, "we still need to tell people that money isn't everything. There are more important things. But it'll be a lot easier for them to focus on the important stuff if they're not worried about money."

"I *think* I'm following you."

"I'm just saying, they'll be a lot more inclined to listen to us if we tell them how to make more money."

"You want us to become self-help gurus? You're the one who said they made pigeons out of their readers."

"Sure," she said, "they do. Because they're trying to get rich. That's why you can't trust them." She looked at me slyly. "But suppose there were someone who knew how to get rich, who was famous for his investment insights, but who wanted to stay poor. Someone whose integrity is guaranteed—with a vow of poverty."

AND SO IT came to pass that the Abbot's Executive Retreat Center actually became a center for executive retreats. The answer had been there in front of us all along. Before long, we were booked solidly with executives eager for inspiration and motivation in a quiet, bucolic monastery with a famous name. Cana became the hot place for corporate retreats. Wall Street traders wanted to know the story of how Our Broker had saved Cana. They also loved the fact that the monastery had been the center of scandal. Brother Bob, who handled reservations, told me that the mergers and acquisitions crowd always asked for the Abbot's own cell. Our high-powered clients were willing to pay handsomely to undergo a few days of monastic routine, and even a little mortification. They did, however, insist on good wine from the Abbot's old cellar.

Our days were busier than ever. The executives rose before dawn and joined us for morning prayers. After an austere but nourishing breakfast, I gave my retreat talk, entitled "The Seven Laws of Spiritual *and* Financial Growth." In the late mornings, there were special workshops for the many executives struggling to overcome their addiction to self-help books and motivational seminars. Brother Gene was positively ruthless on the former Robbinities. Brother Theo was gentler—but highly effective—with the recovering Coveyans. Early afternoons were devoted to teamwork building through such activities as rock climbing on Mount Cana, the bramble-obstacle course, and white-water rafting down the former Cask-Ade. After that, it was chores, followed by a fine dinner prepared by Frère Philippe, our newest monk, then Gregorian chant, meditation, and, finally, the sleep of the just.

Late afternoons, when our clients were busy at their chores, scrubbing the marble floors and tending the gardens, I would take long walks through Cana's former vineyards with Sister Philomena, our Director of Executive Development. One day as we watched the sun set from the top of Mount Cana, we were discussing the idea of expanding— our waiting list for retreatants was now eight months, and growing. We didn't want Cana to become overbuilt and overcrowded. At the same time, we didn't want to turn away the people who sought the Cana experience and the wisdom of the Seven Laws. It was then, looking down on the spot where we had made the bonfire, that Philomena suggested the idea for this book. I resisted at first, but she said it wasn't fair that we should share our wisdom only with the well-to-do.

And so it was that I discovered the Final Law, an amendment to our Seventh Law—"The only way to get rich from a get-rich book is to write one"...

VII ½

...OR BUY THIS ONE.

Market Meditation
the Seventh and a Half

Where can I buy more copies of this wonderful book?
Is there a limit on the number I can purchase?
If my bookstore has already run out due to
overwhelming demand, where can I find more—right away?
(Hint: call 800-733-3000. Or check www.randomhouse.com.)
How can I show my appreciation for the author,
beyond paying full price for the book?

These are your best questions yet! Congratulations! You have truly grown spiritually. The financial part is sure to come!

Now, one final exercise before you "go out there and knock 'em dead." Take a very big piece of paper—in fact, a whole pad. Write down the name of every human being you know. Go through the Rolodex. Find that pile of business cards you never got around to organizing. Take out your alumni directory. Get out the phone book. Don't forget anyone! If in doubt, write it down!

Now, call the bank. Ask them how much money you have left. Call your credit-card companies and find out what your limit is. Do this for every card in your wallet. Are you forgetting any? What about that old MasterCard in the bottom of the drawer? Find out if you can use your gasoline credit cards to buy books. Okay, ready? Let's "grow"!

Go to the nearest bookstore. Bring this book and the list. Give the list and all credit cards—don't forget that Master-

Card!—to the clerk and say, "I want to send this book to everyone on the list, and I want to pay full price" (very important).

Is the clerk smiling at you? Have you made a new friend? See how good it feels to grow?

Prayer of
the Prolific Book Buyer

*Lord, who wrote "The Good Book" and dialed Thy
humble servant Brother Ty and dictated unto
him not only hot stock tips, but also the wisdom contained
in this, the book in my hands, grant that I might
always grow financially, as well as spiritually, and that
I might always have the courage—and the
credit—to buy more copies of this book, as well as any
audiocassettes, calendars, videotapes, bumper stickers,
T-shirts—firkin or otherwise—resulting therefrom,
unto the seventh and a half generation. And if
Thou findest me now standing in the bookstore, browsing
in these pages, hoping to steal away their wisdom
without paying for it, then sendeth me straight to Thy cash
register, that I might render unto the author that
which is, verily, his.*

Amen!

ABOUT THE TYPE

The text of this book is set in Pitt, a typeface designed by Brother Pitt of Harding, an English monk in the Order of Saint Thaddeus. In 1435, bored with the endless copying by hand of illuminated manuscripts, Brother Pitt fabricated movable type and invented the printing press. (A German visiting the monastery, Johann Gutenberg, stole the equipment and used it to produce the first printed Bible.) Brother Pitt designed his typeface for an edition of the monastic order's guiding text, *De Doloribus Extremis*. The bar crossing the "t" is in the shape of the saw used to martyr Saint Thaddeus. The winged serifs symbolize the saint's ascent into heaven. The vertical line through the capital "s" symbolizes the aspirations of the authors with respect to this work.

ABOUT THE AUTHOR

BROTHER TY is the nickname of a monk of the Order of Saint Thaddeus in upstate New York. Before becoming a monk, he was a trader at several prominent Wall Street brokerage houses.

In preparing his book, he was assisted by Christopher Buckley and John Tierney, who are both devout followers of the Seven and a Half Laws.™ Buckley is the best-selling author of *Thank You for Smoking* and a frequent contributor to the *New Yorker*. Tierney is a columnist for the *New York Times*.

HarperPerennial

Books by Christopher Buckley

THANK YOU FOR SMOKING
ISBN 0-06-097662-4

A Public Relations guru takes on the unpopular job of defending the rights of smokers in this biting novel which spoofs political correctness, incorrectness, and the Washington establishment.

"A savagely funny satirical farce."   —*New York Times*

NATIONAL BESTSELLER

WRY MARTINIS
ISBN 0-06-097742-6

A brutally hilarious collection of essays humoring American politics, society, and culture—from the fictitious Clinton-Bush presidential debate to the history of the miniskirt.

"Read this book and you'll die laughing."   —Tom Wolfe

GOD IS MY BROKER
A Monk-Tycoon Reveals the 7 1/2 Laws of Spiritual and *Financial Growth*™
Brother Ty with Christopher Buckley and John Tierney
ISBN 0-06-097761-2

A Wall Street broker joins a monastery after losing all his clients' money in this riotous and first truly great self-help business novel in which ancient texts, inner peace, and financial success finally meet.

"A hilarious book—sly, smart and deeply satisfying."   —*New York Times*

A *NEW YORK TIMES* NOTABLE BOOK

**Available at bookstores everywhere,
or call 1-800-331-3761 to order.**